The Vault/
Investment Bank
is made possible through
the generous support
of the following sponsors:

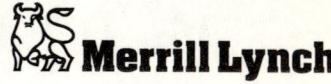

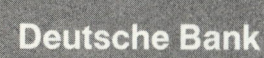 

Goldman Sachs

WACHOVIA
Uncommon Wisdom

LEHMAN BROTHERS

The media's watching Vault!
Here's a sampling of our coverage.

"For those hoping to climb the ladder of success, [Vault's] insights are priceless."
– *Money magazine*

"The best place on the web to prepare for a job search."
– *Fortune*

"[Vault guides] make for excellent starting points for job hunters and should be purchased by academic libraries for their career sections [and] university career centers."
– *Library Journal*

"The granddaddy of worker sites."
– *U.S. News & World Report*

"A killer app."
– *New York Times*

One of Forbes' 33 "Favorite Sites"
– *Forbes*

"To get the unvarnished scoop, check out Vault."
– *SmartMoney Magazine*

"Vault has a wealth of information about major employers and job-searching strategies as well as comments from workers about their experiences at specific companies."
– *The Washington Post*

"Vault has become the go-to source for career preparation."
– *Crain's New York*

"Vault [provides] the skinny on working conditions at all kinds of companies from current and former employees."
– *USA Today*

Rewarding careers with global opportunities.
It starts with you.

UBS is one of the world's leading financial firms, employing over 68,000 people in 50 countries. Our wealth management, global asset management and investment banking businesses offer clients a wide range of products and services designed to help them meet their individual needs and goals.

We seek highly talented individuals who can bring something different to our organization and offer them superb career opportunities to match their potential.

Our people reflect a diversity of views and cultures that is unique in the industry. UBS is committed to an open and meritocratic environment where every employee has the opportunity to thrive and excel, supported by some of the best development and training programs in the industry.

It starts with you.

www.ubs.com/graduates

UBS is an equal opportunity employer committed to diversity in its workforce.

Wealth Management | Global Asset Management | Investment Bank

You & Us

© UBS 2005. All rights reserved.

VAULT/SEO GUIDE TO INVESTMENT BANK DIVERSITY PROGRAMS

© 2005 Vault Inc.

YOU COULD REACH FOR THE MOON.

BUT WHY STOP THERE?

Stars, like people, have differences. But what they do have in common are energy, fire, brilliance – and limitless possibilities.

Merrill Lynch is proud to be a firm that offers exceptional people everywhere their opportunity to shine. By encouraging collaboration between people of different backgrounds and expertise, we're able to create smarter solutions for clients — and put our firm at the very center of the financial universe.

Consider this your invitation to be brilliant with us.

EXCEPTIONAL WITHOUT EXCEPTION

Merrill Lynch is an equal opportunity employer.

ml.com/careers
ml.com/about/diversity

VAULT/SEO GUIDE TO
INVESTMENT BANK DIVERSITY PROGRAMS

THE STAFF OF VAULT

© 2005 Vault Inc.

Copyright © 2005 by Vault Inc. All rights reserved.

All information in this book is subject to change without notice. Vault makes no claims as to the accuracy and reliability of the information contained within and disclaims all warranties. No part of this book may be reproduced or transmitted in any form or by any means, electronic or mechanical, for any purpose, without the express written permission of Vault Inc.

Vault, the Vault logo, and "the most trusted name in career information™" are trademarks of Vault Inc.

For information about permission to reproduce selections from this book, contact Vault Inc., 150 West 22nd St, New York, New York 10011, (212) 366-4212.

Library of Congress CIP Data is available.

ISBN 1-58131-367-5

Printed in the United States of America

Acknowledgments

Many thanks to the members of the committee of representatives from top investment banks who helped us finalize this survey. Vault and SEO would like to thank Margot Medved of Banc of America Securities, Tanji Dewberry of CSFB, Nebal Fahed of Deutsche Bank, Martin Rodriguez of Goldman Sachs, Keith Yardley of HSBC, Mark Chamberlain of JPMorgan Chase, Suzanne Richards and Dimple Dhiman of Lehman Brothers, Keith Webb of Merrill Lynch, and Donald Franklin of UBS for their help on this project.

This book could not have been written without the extraordinary efforts of Woodwyn Koons. We are extremely grateful to Vault's entire staff for all their help in the editorial, production and marketing processes. Vault also would like to acknowledge the support of our investors, clients, employees, family and friends. Thank you!

Special thanks to all of the diversity coordinators and communications representatives who helped with the book. We appreciate your patience with our repeated requests and tight deadlines.

Our momentum is your advantage.

Powered by the financial strength of the fifth-most profitable company in the world, Bank of America's Global Capital Markets and Investment Banking business continues to significantly increase in market share. We work with 97% of the U.S. Fortune 500, we're consistently moving up in underwriting league tables, and we're investing $675 million to grow our business even further.

Our extraordinary momentum creates an invaluable advantage for those who join us. You'll play a key role on our team, one that goes far beyond the typical analyst experience. You'll have greater visibility and more interaction with clients and senior management. And you'll have numerous opportunities to excel as you build an impressive career.

For more details, visit our website.

bofa.com/careers

We are an equal opportunity employer.   The information contained above is based on Bank of America Internal Data.

Table of Contents

INTRODUCTION 1

Letter from William Goodloe 2
SEO Career Program 4
How to Use This Guide 6
Firms Invited to Take the Survey 9
Vault/SEO Letter to Investment Banks 10
Vault/SEO Investment Bank Diversity Survey 12

DIVERSITY PROFILES 21

A. G. Edwards & Sons, Inc. 23
Banc of America Securities 27
Barclays Capital 39
Bear, Stearns & Co., Inc. 45
Brown Brothers Harriman & Co. 49
CIBC World Markets 57
Citigroup 59
Credit Suisse First Boston 75
Deutsche Bank 99
Goldman, Sachs & Co 103
Harris (a part of BMO Financial Group) 115
JPMorgan Chase 127
Lehman Brothers 139
Merrill Lynch & Co. 155
Morgan Stanley 163
TD Securities 181
UBS Investment Bank 187

*Employers highlighted above provided generous underwriting support for the Vault/SEO Guide to Investment Bank Diversity Programs.

xi

Vault/SEO Guide to Investment Bank Diversity Programs
Table of Contents

Wachovia 197

William Blair & Company 201

DIVERSITY DIRECTORY   203

ABN AMRO Holding N.V. 205

Allen & Company 207

Blackstone Group, The 208

BNP Paribas Group 211

Calyon Securities (USA) Inc. 213

Cascadia Capital 215

Chanin Capital Partners 217

Dresdner Kleinwort Wasserstein 219

First Albany Companies 221

Friedman Billings Ramsey 222

Gleacher Partners 225

Greenhill & Co. 227

Houlihan Lokey Howard & Zukin 229

HSBC Bank USA 231

Jefferies & Co. 234

Keefe, Bruyette & Woods 235

KeyCorp 236

Lazard Limited 240

Legg Mason Wood Walker, Inc. 243

Morgan Keegan & Co. 246

National City 248

Nomura Holdings 250

Piper Jaffray 251

Putnam Lovell NBF Securities Inc. 253

Raymond James Financial 255

*Employers highlighted above provided generous underwriting support for the Vault/SEO Guide to Investment Bank Diversity Programs.

RBC Capital Markets 257
Robert W. Baird & Co. (Baird) .... (b259
Rothschild North America 261
Ryan Beck & Company 263
Sandler O'Neill 265
SG Cowen & Co., LLC 267
Stephens Inc. 269
Susquehanna International Group 271
Thomas Weisel Partners 273
Veronis Suhler Stevenson 275
WR Hambrecht + Co. 277

About the Authors 280

what
- Accounting
- Asset Management
- Global Corporate Finance
- Corporate Law
- Information Technology
- Investment Banking
- Management Consulting
- Philanthropy

who

ABFE | A.T. Kearney | Banc of America Securities | Barclays | Blackrock | Carnegie Corporation of New York | Citigroup | Cleary, Gottlieb, Steen & Hamilton | Clifford Chance | Cravath, Swaine & Moore | Credit Suisse First Boston | Davis Polk & Wardwell | Deutsche Bank | Deutsche Bank Americas Foundation | Edwin Gould Foundation for Children | Fried, Frank, Harris, Shriver & Jacobson | Goldman, Sachs & Co. | Hispanics in Philanthropy | IBM | Jessie Smith-Noyes Foundation | JPMorgan | Lazard Ltd | LeBoeuf, Lamb, Greene & MacRae | Lehman Brothers | Merrill Lynch | Milbank, Tweed Hadley & McCloy | Monitor Group | Morgan, Lewis & Bockius | Morgan Stanley | New York Regional Association of Grantmakers | Paul, Weiss, Rifkind, Wharton & Garrison | Rockefeller Brothers Fund | Rockefeller Philanthropy Advisors | Shearman & Sterling | Simpson Thacher & Bartlett | Skadden, Arps, Slate, Meagher & Flom | Sullivan & Cromwell | Teagle Foundation | The Boston Consulting Group | UBS | Wachtell, Lipton, Rosen & Katz | Wallace Foundation | Weil, Gotshal & Manges | Xerox

Have a challenging, high-paying job waiting for you on graduation day

Earn $600 – $1,100 a week in a Mentored Summer Internship

For 25 years, Sponsors for Educational Opportunity (SEO) has offered mentored internships to outstanding college students of color — Black, Hispanic/Latino, Asian and Native American. Start building a solid career path as early as your sophomore year in college. All you need is a 3.0 GPA and a hunger to compete for what could be your opportunity of a lifetime.

apply now!

application deadlines | November 1st Early action 1 | December 15th Early action 2 | January 15th Fin
apply online | www.seo-usa.org

Introduction

Vault is proud to partner with Sponsors for Educational Opportunity (SEO), a top nonprofit organization that trains and develops talented minority youth for professional careers in business and industry, on the first annual edition of the *Vault/SEO Guide to Investment Bank Diversity Programs*. Vault and SEO make ideal partners to bring students, young professionals and educators the most recent, accurate and up-to-date information on investment bank diversity planning, representation, strategies and programs.

For this first annual *Guide*, 20 investment banks shared their actions and goals in the crucial area of corporate diversity in self-reported profiles. By participating in the *Guide*, companies are not necessarily endorsing Vault or SEO, and there is no requirement that they be, have been or plan to be an SEO partner. Rather, they are expressing their commitment to, and appreciation of, the importance of diversity in the 21st century workplace.

We also have included a directory of other top banks that chose not to submit a self-reported profile. The information in these directory entries is basic employment and, where publicly available, diversity information. Again, inclusion in the Guide or the directory should not be taken as an endorsement of Vault or SEO.

We thank all the participants in the first *Vault/SEO Guide to Investment Bank Diversity Programs* and we hope that its readers will find it instructive and useful in evaluating and benchmarking potential employers, peers and partners.

The Editors
Vault, Inc.

Letter from William Goodloe

Dear Reader,

In the last few decades, the mission to increase diversity in investment banking has grown from a small, uncertain enterprise to a mainstream practice integral to the recruitment strategies of the leading firms on Wall Street. At SEO, we have been invested in this mission for 25 years, and it is with delight and pride that we introduce this inaugural edition of the *Vault/SEO Guide to Investment Bank Diversity Programs*.

The SEO Career Program was founded in 1980 with the support of a number of Wall Street visionaries, in particular John Whitehead, then Co-Chairman of Goldman Sachs. That first summer, we started small, placing 11 minority interns with four banks. We had no guarantee of success - in fact, many doubted whether our interns would be prepared to succeed in the competitive atmosphere of investment banking.

By the end of that summer, all 11 interns received full-time job offers from their firms. Since then, the SEO Career Program has grown beyond our expectations to become Wall Street's single largest source of recent college graduate hires at the analyst level. In 2005, the Career Program placed 250 interns of color from 66 colleges at 12 investment banks in New York, San Francisco and Hong Kong. If the previous year is any guide, these interns will receive full-time job offers from their firms at virtually the same rate as students recruited directly by the firms from the best colleges in the nation.

Although diversity recruitment can truly be said to have entered the mainstream of corporate thinking, much progress remains to be made. The *Vault/SEO Guide to Investment Bank Diversity Programs* will provide an invaluable source of information to both firms and students alike. With this guide, firms will be able to examine the diversity programs and initiatives of their fellow firms, share best practices and use the information gathered here as a benchmark against which to measure their own diversity efforts.

Copies of this guide will also be available at colleges across the nation, allowing talented students of color who are considering a career in the field to make informed decisions in applying for internships and full-time jobs. The number of talented students across the nation is greater than any single organization can hope to reach. This guide will be crucial in expanding the information available to all interested firms and students everywhere.

Finally, if your company is seeking to expand its diversity efforts, we at SEO will be happy to explore how partnering with us can be an effective way to bring highly talented and motivated interns of color into your firm. In addition, to augment your lateral hiring efforts, we can help you reach more than 2,000 SEO alumni who have gained valuable training and experience at our nation's most successful investment banks. Details on how to contact SEO are included in this directory.

For all of us dedicated to building and strengthening diversity programs in investment banking, this guide will be a great resource. We hope you enjoy it.

Sincerely,

William A. Goodloe

William A. Goodloe
President, SEO

SEO Career Program

SPONSORS FOR EDUCATIONAL OPPORTUNITY (SEO) is the nation's premier summer internship program for talented students of color. The SEO Career Program has expanded from 11 interns placed at four investment banks in 1980 to serving hundreds of exceptional students of color annually. SEO interns are placed in eight of the nation's most competitive industries, including investment banking, corporate law, asset management, global corporate finance, management consulting, information technology, accounting and philanthropy. Since its inception, the SEO Career Program has placed nearly 4,000 Black, Hispanic/Latino, Asian and Native American students in rigorous internships leading to full full-time job offers. In recent years, more than 80% of SEO Career Program interns have received job offers from SEO partner firms after their internships.

The SEO Investment Banking Program continues to grow. In 2005, 250 SEO interns were placed in summer analyst positions in corporate finance, sales & trading, research, asset management and public finance in New York, San Francisco, Stamford, Ct., and Hong Kong. SEO now has 12 investment banking partners: Banc of America Securities; Barclays Capital; Citigroup; Credit Suisse First Boston; Deutsche Bank; Goldman Sachs; JPMorgan; Lazard Ltd.; Lehman Brothers; Merrill Lynch; Morgan Stanley and UBS.

THE ORIENTATION AND TRAINING that SEO Career Program interns receive prepares them to not only meet, but exceed, their greatest expectations for professional performance and personal growth during their summer internships. SEO partners with Zoologic, a leader in Web-based learning for financial professionals, and Training the Street, which provides live instruction in financial modeling and valuation, as well as renowned professors from the best business schools in the country, to offer interns a comprehensive skills training program before their internships begin. In addition, the SEO Summer Seminar Series, featuring presentations by the CEOs and presidents of our investment banking partners, offers interns the chance to meet, learn from and stay in contact with managing directors, partners and recruiting officers from SEO partner firms.

MENTORING AND ALUMNI SUPPORT are also integral to the success of the SEO Career Program. SEO provides industry and alumni mentors to all of its interns, who help students navigate through their industry, overcome specific job challenges, balance professional and personal concerns and convert their internships into full-time job offers. In addition, SEO Career Program interns graduate into a powerful network of thousands of SEO alumni in 43 states and 30 countries. SEO alumni are not only thriving professionally but serving their communities as board members, financial contributors, mentors and volunteers. Combined, these resources put SEO interns on the fast track to some of the most financially and personally rewarding career opportunities in the world.

For more information on the SEO Career Program, please visit our website at: www.seo-usa.org. To explore joining SEO as a corporate partner, please contact Julian Johnson, Senior Vice President, at 212-979-2040 or via email at jjohnson@seo-usa.org.

How to Use this Guide

Over the past few years, most U.S. companies have devoted increasing resources to diversity initiatives as well as to the management and administration of these efforts. Nearly all have developed their own unique approach and method of administration. This book was developed to provide students with the essential objective information necessary to meaningfully evaluate investment banks' diversity initiatives and programs, as well as allow investment banks to benchmark their efforts against their peer firms. We hope that the information contained within this guide will enable students to match their interests and career objectives with an appropriate company.

The guide format presents the same information for all banks in a user-friendly way, addressing the degree to which several widely-recognized "best practices" are being incorporated into the bank's diversity program.

The complete survey sent to the company is printed in the Guide. In cases where a bank did not respond to a question, the unanswered question is not reprinted in that bank's profile; that question is simply left out. For questions where banks had the option of choosing one or more options to answer a question, we listed the choices the bank chose; to see which answers the bank did not choose, you can refer to the full text of the survey.

We encourage you to use the information in the guide as a springboard to ask constructive questions and open a dialogue that will empower you to define your relationship with the bank. In the case of students evaluating potential employers, it may be whether the bank's efforts measure up to your personal goals and developmental needs.

If a bank was invited but chose not to participate, that bank was included in the directory at the back of this book with basic hiring contact information, and, where available, diversity information from the bank's web site. Inclusion in this directory should not be taken as approval of the *Guide*.

The survey was developed with the advice and assistance of representatives from nine investment banks (Banc of America Securities, Credit Suisse First Boston, Deutsche Bank, Goldman Sachs, HSBC, JPMorgan, Lehman Brothers, Merrill Lynch and UBS).

Definitions

The survey refers to full-time or permanent exempt employees in the U.S. Entry-level college graduate hires are new full-time, professional hires made directly from undergraduate institutions. Exempt employees are employees who are not temporary, hourly or contract.

For this survey, diversity is defined as male and female minorities and white women but does not include gay and lesbian employees.

For this survey, minorities are defined as those whose race is other than White/Caucasian (e.g., African-American/Black, Latino/Hispanic, Asian and Native American).

Firm Contact Info

This section contains basic information, including the contact person for diversity hiring. Offices and revenues, also in this section, give a sense of the size of the bank – some would-be bankers prefer larger banks, while others prefer more intimate boutiques.

Strategic Plan and Diversity Leadership

Once a bank has committed to work at being more diverse, there are various ways in which the bank can advance that commitment. It may be helpful for the reader to pay attention to what steps the bank's management has taken to communicate its diversity commitment widely and to develop a clear action plan for progress. Is diversity progress a goal that has been set with bank-wide responsibility and accountability? Do diversity leaders have a voice on management issues? You can begin to explore some of those issues in this section.

Recruitment

Here's where you find out how to get hired at the bank of your choice. This section contains useful information on schools at which the bank recruits (for new analysts) as well as other outreach efforts, including participation in conferences, career panels and scholarship programs. Similar information is available for professional hires, as well as insight on whether the bank uses women and/or minority-owned executive search firms to make hires.

Internships

Internships are a key way to be hired by any top investment bank. This section describes the type of internship programs (there may be more than one) offered by the bank, as well as contact information.

Scholarships

Many banks offer special scholarship programs for qualified minority students. You'll find the details, including the amount, the deadline to apply and contact information in this section for banks that offer scholarships.

Affinity groups/Employee networks

If you're thinking of joining a bank, either as a new analyst or a more experienced associate, you may wish to join an affinity group or employee network, which is an internal organization that addresses the needs and interests of specific minority groups (sometimes including women and gays, lesbians, bisexuals and transexuals).

Entry-level programs/Full-time opportunities/Training programs

Looking for a place to work after graduation that may differ from the place where you did your internship. This section gives an overview of the type of entry-level positions at the bank, including training and any kind of educational perks (like tuition reimbursement).

Diversity statement

Many banks have a kind of guiding credo that shapes their approach to employment diversity issues; you'll find it in this section (if the bank has one.)

Additional information

This section of the bank's diversity profile is comprised of a narrative composed by the bank. There were no requirements regarding what had to be addressed (although we admit to having made a few suggestions). This section offers a great place for the bank to elaborate on some of its answers to the survey questions and discuss things they are doing that we may have failed to cover.

In conclusion, we hope that this book assists you in identifying banks that are a good match to your diversity values and needs. Remember: although you can get a quick impression by flipping through these pages and looking at diversity program overviews, and yes/no responses, the most important factor is the commitment of the bank to diversity goals. We hope you find what you're looking for in this Guide.

Firms Invited to Take the Survey

A.G. Edwards & Sons, Inc.
ABN AMRO Holdings
Allen & Company
Banc of America Securities
Barclays Capital
Bear Stearns
Blackstone Group
BNP Paribas
Brown Brothers Harriman & Co.
Calyon Securities
Cascadia Capital LLC
Chanin Capital Partners
CIBC World Markets
Citigroup's Global Corporate and Investment Bank
Credit Suisse First Boston
Deutsche Bank
Dresdner Kleinwort Wasserstein
First Albany Companies
Friedman Billings Ramsey
Gleacher Partners
Goldman Sachs
Greenhill & Co.
Harris Nesbitt
Houlihan Lokey Howard & Zukin
HSBC
Jefferies & Company
JPMorgan Chase
Keefe, Bruyette & Woods

KeyCorp
Lazard Ltd..
Legg Mason
Lehman Brothers
Merrill Lynch
Morgan Keegan & Company
Morgan Stanley
National City
Nomura Holdings
Peter J. Solomon Company
Piper Jaffray & Co.
Putnam Lovell NBF Securities Inc.
Raymond James Financial
RBC Capital Markets
Robert W. Baird (Baird)
Rothschild
Ryan Beck & Co., Inc.
Sandler O'Neill
SG Cowen & Co., LLC
Stephens Inc.
Susquehanna International Group
TD Securities
Thomas Weisel Partners
UBS Investment Bank
Veronis Suhler Stevenson
Wachovia Corporation
William Blair & Company, LLC
WR Hambrecht + Co

Vault/SEO Letter to Investment Banks

We are writing to alert you to a very exciting project and to ask for your involvement in what promises to be an effective means to bring together information on activities of investment banks in the critical area of diversity.

SEO, a key educational and career resource for young people of color, and Vault Inc., a premier source of employment information for MBAs, JDs, college students and grad students, have partnered to develop the attached Investment Bank Diversity Survey. We finalized the survey with the advice and assistance of a committee of representatives from nine investment banks (Banc of America Securities, CSFB, Deutsche Bank, Goldman Sachs, HSBC, JP Morgan Chase, Lehman Brothers, Merrill Lynch, UBS). We are requesting that all firms listed below complete the survey, which we believe represents the best way to inform students and career officers of diversity initiatives, stimulate diversity progress and achieve a measure of consistency in how diversity information is reported.

Vault will compile all of the completed surveys into a directory called the *Vault/SEO Guide to Investment Bank Diversity Programs*. The guide's purpose is to educate interested students, recent graduates and career officers, as well as the investment bank community, on the commitment and types of diversity programs in place at over 50 large and prestigious investment banking firms (see list below). The objectives of publishing the guide are:

- To introduce students and career officers to the wide range of diversity initiatives and opportunities available for students of color at each participating organization;

- To provide a consistent profile of current investment bank diversity planning, implementation and representation;

- To identify the best practices for the design and implementation of diversity initiatives in investment banks; and

- To outline the strategies, programs, and metrics that investment banks use to increase the recruitment, retention and promotion of minority and women employees.

This guide is similar to some of Vault's other publications, such as the *Vault/MCCA Guide to Law Firm Diversity Programs*, in two significant ways:

- **All information is self-reported by each firm**. Each firm's data will be published virtually as submitted, with only minor editing from Vault for clarity and length, and all edits will be reviewed and approved by the firm prior to publication.

- **There are no rankings**. Rather, Vault is simply gathering and presenting information about each firm's diversity efforts. Firm profiles will appear in alphabetical order.

The Vault/SEO Guide to Investment Bank Diversity Programs will be distributed free of charge to every firm that submits a completed survey and to the career center offices of approximately 500 colleges and universities in the United States.

We hope that you will join us in this effort by completing and returning the attached survey by **May 2, 2005**.

If you have any questions, please direct them to SEO's SVP, Julian Johnson, at (646) 435-9172 or jjohnson@seo-usa.org, or Vault's VP of Content, Marcy Lerner at (212) 366-3724 or mlerner@staff.vault.com.

Best regards,

William Goodloe
President & CEO
www.seo-usa.org

Samer Hamadeh
Co-founder & CEO, Vault
www.vault.com

Vault/SEO Investment Bank Diversity Survey

Survey Introduction

Welcome to the inaugural effort of the *Vault/SEO Guide to Investment Bank Diversity Programs* (2006 Edition). In anticipation of questions and comments regarding this survey, we have prepared the following instruction sheet to guide you. Of course, if you still have questions, please do not hesitate to contact us at the phone numbers and e-mail addresses below.

We thank you for your understanding and welcome comments and feedback as we seek to improve the survey for future editions.

The Process

Participation is entirely free of charge. We ask that a representative or group of representatives from your firm complete the attached questionnaire (in MS Word format) within the next five weeks. You are free to skip any question that you do not wish to answer, but we encourage you to be as thorough as possible. Please note that each firm should complete and return only one questionnaire. Do not handwrite or PDF survey responses. Please e-mail the completed questionnaire to editor Woodwyn Koons at wkoons@vault.com. You may also call SEO's SVP, Julian Johnson, at (646) 435-9572 or Marcy Lerner, Vault's VP of Content, at (212) 366-3724 with any questions.

Distribution

The Vault/SEO Guide to Investment Bank Diversity Programs will be distributed free of charge to every bank that submits a completed survey, to over 1,000 former and current SEO interns, and to the undergraduate career office of approximately 500 colleges and universities in the United States. The guide will also be sold through college and university bookstores and on the Internet. Excerpts from the Guide will also be available free at www.vault.com. At no additional charge, moreover, the entire Guide will be available to Vault Gold subscribers and to the 500-plus colleges and universities worldwide that have subscribed to the Vault Online Career Library.

Instructions

Format

1. You may opt not to answer any question on the survey.

2. Please provide all answers in Word via e-mail. Do not fax or PDF your completed surveys.

Global Definitions

1. The survey refers to full-time or permanent exempt employees in the U.S. Entry-level college graduate hires are new full-time, professional or white-collar hires made directly from undergraduate institutions. Exempt employees are employees who are not temporary, hourly or contract.

2. For this survey, diversity is defined as male and female minorities and white women but does not include gay and lesbian employees.

3. For this survey, minorities are defined as those whose race is other than White/Caucasian (e.g., African-American/Black, Latino/Hispanic, Asian and Native American).

Section I.

For locations, please list all worldwide locations with an investment bank function.

Section VI.

Though this survey does not include GLBT employees for the purposes of minority definition, you may choose to list any GLBT affinity groups in this section.

Section IX.

In the narrative, some points you may address or provide include:

- More detail on diversity scholarships for interns, co-ops or entry-level college hires

- More detail on part-time/flex-time programs

- More detail on the workings of your diversity committee

- The names of the minority associations with which you have relationships and the nature of those relationships

- List and description of diversity awards and honors

- How the firm has communicated to partners the link between diversity and business success

- If the firm provides financial support or services to minority public interest organizations and if so, the name of those organizations

- The nature and scope of the firm's Equal Employment Opportunity and Prevention of Harassment policy

- If the firm ties progress on diversity initiatives to compensation in any way

I. Firm Contact Info

Contact Person: _____ Title: _____

Diversity Team Leader/Diversity Campus Recruiting Team Leader: (name & title)
_____

Firm Name: _____

Address: _____

City: _____ State: _____ Zip: _____

Phone: _____ Fax: _____ E-mail: _____

Office Locations (worldwide): _____
_____

2004 Revenues (U.S.) _____ Total (Worldwide) _____

Web site address for diversity _____

II. Strategic Plan and Diversity Leadership

1. How does the firm's leadership communicate the importance of diversity to everyone at the firm? (e.g., e-mails, web site, newsletters, meetings, etc.) _____
_____

2. (a) Who has primary responsibility for leading overall diversity initiatives at your firm? Name of person and his/her title: _____

(b) Who has primary responsibility for diversity recruiting initiatives at your firm, if different from (a)? Name of person and his/her title: _____

3. (a) Does your firm currently have a diversity committee? ☐ Yes   ☐ No

(b) If yes, does the committee's representation include one or more members of the firm's management/executive committee (or the equivalent)? ☐ Yes   ☐ No

(c) If yes, how many senior managers are on the committee, and how often did the committee convene in furtherance of the firm's diversity initiatives in 2004?)

Total senior managers on committee: _____

Number of diversity meetings annually: _____

(d) If you have more than one diversity committee, please list. _____
_____

4. Does the committee(s) and/or diversity leader establish and set goals or objectives consistent with management's priorities?

Yes ☐   No ☐   Partially (explain): ☐ _____

5. Has the firm undertaken a formal or informal diversity program or set of initiatives aimed at increasing the diversity of the firm?

Yes, formal ☐   Yes, informal ☐   No ☐

6. (a) How often does the firm's management review the firm's diversity progress/results?

☐   Monthly

☐   Quarterly

☐   Twice a year

☐   Annually

☐   Does not review/measure progress/results

☐   Other, please specify _____

(b) How is the firm's diversity committee(s) and/or firm management held accountable for achieving results? _____

7. Are the members of the diversity committee or committees involved in diversity activities? ☐ Yes   ☐ No

If so, list and describe some of those activities.

III. Recruitment of New Analysts and Associates

On-campus

8. Does your firm annually recruit at any of the following types of institutions? (Check all that apply and list the schools).

- ☐ Ivy League schools:_____
- ☐ Public state schools:_____
- ☐ Private schools:_____
- ☐ Historically Black Colleges and Universities (HBCUs): _____
- ☐ Hispanic Serving Institutions (HSIs):_____
- ☐ Native American Tribal Universities: _____
- ☐ Other predominantly minority and/or women's colleges: _____

9. Of the schools that you listed above, do you have any special outreach efforts directed to encourage minority students to consider your firm?

- ☐ Hold a reception for minority students
- ☐ Conferences   Please list _____
- ☐ Advertise in minority student association publication(s)
- ☐ Participate in/host minority student job fair(s)
- ☐ Sponsor minority student association events
- ☐ Firm's professionals participate on career panels at school
- ☐ Outreach to leadership of minority student organizations
- ☐ Scholarships or intern/fellowships for minority students
- ☐ Other, please specify _____

Professional Recruiting

10. What activities does the firm undertake to attract women and minorities?

- ☐ Partner programs with women and minority banking associations
- ☐ Conferences   Please list_____
- ☐ Participate at minority job fairs

☐ Seek referrals from other professionals

☐ Utilize online job services

☐ Other, please specify _____

(a) Do you use executive recruiting/search firms to seek to identify new diversity hires? ☐ Yes ☐ No

(b) If yes, list all women- and/or minority-owned executive search/recruiting firms to which the firm paid a fee for placement services in the past 12 months: _____
_____

IV. Internships

For the following section, please repeat this template as necessary if you have more than one internship, including those primarily aimed at minority undergraduate students.

Name of internship program (ie, summer analyst program, SEO program) _____

Deadline for application for the internship _____

Number of interns in the program in summer 2004 _____

Pay ($US) _____ (indicate if by week, by month, or for entire program)

Length of the program (in weeks) _____

Percentage of interns in the program who receive offers of full-time employment
_____

Web site for internship information _____

Please describe the internship program, including departments hiring, intern responsibilities, qualifications for the program and any other details you feel are relevant.

V. Scholarships

For the following section, please repeat this template as necessary if you have more than one scholarship aimed at minority undergraduate students.

Name of scholarship program _____

Deadline for application for the scholarship program _____

Scholarship award amount _____

Web site or other contact information for scholarship _____

Please describe the scholarship program, including basic requirements, eligibility, length of program and any other details you feel are relevant.

VI. Affinity Groups

For the following section, please repeat this template as necessary if you have more than one affinity group at your organization.

Name of affinity group _____

Name of affinity group leader (optional) _____

Contact information or web site address for affinity group and/or leader _____

Please describe the affinity group, including its purpose, how often it meets, web site, etc.

VII. Entry-level Programs/Full-time Opportunities/Training Programs

For the following section, please repeat this template as necessary if you have more than one full-time, entry-level, rotational or training program at your organization.

Name of program_____

Length of program_____

Geographic location(s) of program_____

Please describe the training/training component of this program _____

Please describe any other educational components of this program (i.e., tuition reimbursement, mentorship) _____

VIII. Diversity Mission Statement

Please provide your company's diversity mission statement if applicable.

IX. Additional Information

In a narrative of 500 words or less, please provide any additional information regarding your firm's diversity initiatives that you wish to share.

IS THIS YOUR CHAMPIONSHIP SEASON?

Preparation. Great Coaching. Focus. An unrelenting pursuit of victory. That's the stuff of champions.

Introducing Ntential℠, a revolutionary new career development system designed to help you reach your infinite career potential. Whether you're just joining the game, mid-career, changing direction or starting your own enterprise, NBMBAA Ntential℠ offers you:

- A choice among world-class life and career coaches who provide candid, insightful and confidential feedback geared toward moving you ahead.
- 24/7 access to state-of-the-art online resources designed to help you visualize, organize and actualize the game plan for your own championship season.

Ntential℠ is part of a suite of NBMBAA services including Employment Network®, Career Success Network℠ and NBMBAA Leadership Institute that add value to the careers and lives of active professionals every day.

Visit www.nbmbaa.org/ntential to view *Candidates For Success!* the eye-opening stories of six real NBMBAA members who tried Ntential℠ for just three months.

Unlock your potential at www.nbmbaa.org/ntential

INVESTMENT BANK DIVERSITY PROFILES

A. G. Edwards & Sons, Inc.

One N. Jefferson Ave.
St. Louis, MO 63103
Phone: 314-955-3431
E-mail: snyder@agedwards.com

Contact Information

Contact Person: Bill Snyder,
Associate Vice President, Employment

Strategic Plan and Diversity Leadership

How does the firm's leadership communicate the importance of diversity to everyone at the firm?
Annual goal statement from the CEO

Does your firm currently have a diversity committee? No

Has the firm undertaken a formal or informal diversity program or set of initiatives aimed at increasing the diversity of the firm? Yes, formal

How often does the firm's management review the firm's diversity progress/results? Annually

How is the firm's diversity committee(s) and/or firm management held accountable for achieving results?
Periodic review and analysis of demographic data

Recruitment of New Analysts and Associates

On-campus

Please list the schools at which your firm recruits.

- Public state schools
- Private schools
- Historically Black Colleges and Universities (HBCUs)

Professional Recruiting

What activities does the firm undertake to attract women and minorities?

- Participate at minority job fairs
- Seek referrals from other professionals
- Utilize online job services

Do you use executive recruiting/search firms to seek to identify new diversity hires? No

Our momentum is your advantage.

Powered by the financial strength of the fifth-most profitable company in the world, Bank of America's Global Capital Markets and Investment Banking business continues to significantly increase in market share. We work with 97% of the U.S. Fortune 500, we're consistently moving up in underwriting league tables, and we're investing $675 million to grow our business even further.

Our extraordinary momentum creates an invaluable advantage for those who join us. You'll play a key role on our team, one that goes far beyond the typical analyst experience. You'll have greater visibility and more interaction with clients and senior management. And you'll have numerous opportunities to excel as you build an impressive career.

For more details, visit our website.

bofa.com/careers

Bank of America   Higher Standards

We are an equal opportunity employer.   The information contained above is based on Bank of America Internal Data.

Banc of America Securities

9 West 57th Street
New York, NY 10019
www.bofasecurities.com

Locations

Charlotte, NC
New York, NY
San Francisco, CA

Banc of America Securities LLC, a subsidiary of Bank of America Corporation, is a full-service investment bank and brokerage firm with principal offices in Charlotte, New York and San Francisco. Together with its London affiliate, Banc of America Securities Limited, the firm delivers capital raising, financial advisory and risk management solutions, bulge-bracket trading and global distribution services, and objective research on global markets and growth sectors to corporations, institutional investors, financial institutions and government entities.

The Stats

Revenue (2004): $9,049 million (Bank of America Securities)
Revenue (2004): $48,894 million (company-wide)

Bank of America is one of the world's leading financial services companies, with more than $600 billion in assets, 137,000 associates, offices in 35 countries and client solutions spanning 150 countries.

Contact Information

Contact Person: Monika Cox, Senior Vice President, Global Capital Markets and Investment Banking Staffing Executive
Diversity Team Leader/Diversity Campus Recruiting Team Leader: Joanne Franklin
Diversity URL: corp.bankofamerica.com/public/career/diversity.jsp

Strategic Plan and Diversity Leadership

How does the firm's leadership communicate the importance of diversity to everyone at the firm?

The firm's leadership communicates the importance of diversity through the following channels:

- Town Hall meetings
- Presentations
- Corporate and Line of Business intranet sites
- Featured stories
- Brochures
- Conference calls and other meetings
- Brown Bag Luncheons
- Recognition events
- Newsletters
- Leveraging diversity networks and affinity groups
- Intra-company broadcasts
- E-mails
- Diversity web sites
- Newsletters

Who has primary responsibility for leading overall diversity initiatives at your firm?
Geri Thomas, Bank of America Diversity Executive

Who has primary responsibility for diversity recruiting initiatives at your firm, if different from above?
Greg Jones, SVP, Diversity Recruiting – Experienced Recruiting. Campus recruiting is handled by line of business campus recruiting teams.

Does your firm currently have a diversity committee? Yes

If yes, does the committee's representation include one or more members of the firm's management/executive committee (or the equivalent)? Yes

If yes, how many senior managers are on the committee, and how often did the committee convene in furtherance of the firm's diversity initiatives in 2004?

Total senior managers on committee: 27
Number of diversity meetings annually: 4 formal meetings per year, subcommittee meetings may be held as often as weekly

If you have more than one diversity committee, please list.

- Team Bank of America, the bank's associate involvement structure, has local diversity networks. The diversity networks are organized locally by volunteers and work across lines of business on diversity awareness activities.

- Next, there are also many line of business diversity business councils, which work to support the realization of divisional diversity goals. These councils work within individual lines of business and throughout geographical areas, while the Team Bank of America networks are more grassroots and regional.

- Finally, there are developmental groups, which we call affinity groups.

- Currently, there are groups for African Americans, Asian Americans, people with disabilities, Gay/Lesbian/Bisexual/Transgender people, Hispanic/Latino Americans, parents and women.

Does the committee(s) and/or diversity leader establish and set goals or objectives consistent with management's priorities? Yes

Has the firm undertaken a formal or informal diversity program or set of initiatives aimed at increasing the diversity of the firm? Yes, formal

How often does the firm's management review the firm's diversity progress/results?
Statistics are reviewed on a monthly basis and a formal report is sent to the executive board on a quarterly basis.

How are the firm's diversity committee(s) and/or firm management held accountable for achieving results?
Diversity goals are an integral part of our Hoshin plans, the chief strategic document of our business.

Are the members of the diversity committee or committees involved in diversity activities? Yes

Members of the diversity committees set the direction and guide the implementation of diversity and inclusion at Bank of America. These committee members advise dozens of Diversity Business Councils operating in various business lines to address diversity and inclusion issues. Their role is to encourage and capitalize on the diversity of our associates and promote personal and professional development. The committee members also meet with affinity groups periodically to network and support development and success. Finally, the committee members work to ensure that senior executive management develops annual targets to increase diversity in their businesses and have incentive pay tied to progress in hiring, promoting and retaining people of color.

Recruitment of New Analysts and Associates

On-campus

List the schools at which your firm recruits.

- Ivy League schools
- Public state schools
- Private schools
- Historically Black Colleges and Universities (HBCUs)
- Hispanic Serving Institutions (HSIs)
- Native American Tribal Universities
- Other predominantly minority and/or women's colleges

Banc of America Securities formally recruited on the following campuses in 2004:

- Amherst College
- Barnard College
- Boston College
- Cal Tech
- Carnegie Mellon
- Claremont McKenna
- Columbia University
- Cornell University
- Dartmouth
- Davidson

- Duke University
- Emory University
- Florida A&M
- Florida International
- Georgetown University
- Harvey Mudd
- Harvard University
- Howard University
- Indiana
- Johns Hopkins
- James Madison University
- MIT
- Morehouse
- Northwestern University
- NYU
- Rice
- RPI
- Stanford
- Texas A&M
- UC-Berkeley
- UNC-Chapel Hill
- University of Chicago
- University of Illinois
- University of Michigan
- University of Pennsylvania
- University of Southern California
- University of Virginia
- University of Wisconsin
- UT-Austin
- Vanderbilt
- Wake Forest
- Washington University-St. Louis
- Washington & Lee University
- Wellesley
- Yale

Of the schools that you listed above, do you have any special outreach efforts directed to encourage minority students to consider your firm.

- Hold a reception for minority students
- Conferences
- Advertise in minority student association publication(s)
- Participate in/host minority student job fair(s)
- Sponsor minority student association events
- Firm's professionals participate on career panels at school
- Outreach to leadership of minority student organizations
- Scholarships or intern/fellowships for minority students

Internships

Banc of America Securities offers summer internship opportunities in: Corporate & Investment Banking; Capital Markets; Global Markets – Sales & Trading; Research; and Global Portfolio Management. We also offer a small rotational program for rising college juniors. All summer internships are 10 weeks long and kick off with an orientation session. During orientation interns learn some Banc of America Securities' basics: technical skills, our views on the markets and professional practices that will make their summer experience all the more valuable. Training continues throughout the summer as interns participate in presentations and other group and individual projects led by industry experts. Interns also have the opportunity to work closely with professionals throughout our organization including experts in investment banking, sales, trading, origination and research. This is a great opportunity to build a network of colleagues across the firm.

Over the course of the internship, interns will have access to ongoing education to help them achieve expertise in their specific business area. In 2004 we launched the Learning Network, which is a repository of information on all the development opportunities available to employees at Banc of America Securities. By accessing the system interns can enroll in and view all course objectives, logistics and pre-work assigned to the e-learning modules and programs that have been developed for the entry-level population.

For more information on our summer internship programs, please visit: bofa.com/careers.

Affinity Groups/Employee Networks

Bank of America's associate affinity groups are a vital part of the company's diversity and inclusion efforts. The affinity groups are informal, bank-supported groups made up of associates who have a common identity along with others who support them. The groups meet periodically to network and encourage each other's development and success. By giving voice to diverse constituencies within the company and to customers like themselves, the groups assist Bank of America with maintaining a fair and inclusive workplace. They also can enhance the bank's efforts to bring exceptional, targeted products and services to our customers, clients and shareholders.

Any interested associate – regardless of background – is welcome to join one or more of the groups.

The Asian American Leadership Network – The Asian American Leadership Network (AALN) is a resource for any Asian American associate at Bank of America whose aim is to be a successful leader at the company. The AALN has three key focus areas. The first is helping Asian American associates build or improve skills necessary for successful career performance and advancement. Specific activities include mentoring by senior bank executives. Secondly, the AALN reaches out to and becomes active in local Asian American communities. Lastly, through events showcasing and celebrating the diverse cultures of Asia, the AALN team increases awareness and appreciation for these cultures.

The Black Professionals Group – Formerly known as the African-American Networking Initiative, the Black Professionals Group (BPG) has a two-pronged mission: to maximize the contributions of black and African American associates at Bank of America, and to enhance their professional development. In line with its commitment to build the next generation of leaders, the group's activities in the past have included formal mentoring initiatives as well as programs that build the skills needed to progress in a corporate environment. Beyond this emphasis, the BPG also sponsors and promotes opportunities for its members and their supporters to network with one another and with the broader communities inside and outside of Bank of America.

Bank of America Pride Resource Group – The mission of the Bank of America PRIDE Resource Group is to make the bank the most admired company of gay, lesbian, bisexual and transgender (GLBT) associates, consumers and investors. The group aims to accomplish that task by promoting a safe and equitable workplace for

GLBT associates and fostering a work environment that will attract and retain the best GLBT talent.

PRIDE serves as a resource to its members and all levels of management by focusing on issues important to the GLBT community and by organizing activities for its members and allies to meet, network, and support one another. To further serve the corporation, PRIDE works to promote brand awareness and market development opportunities within the GLBT community through the coordination of and participation in diversity events, conferences, marketing efforts and recruiting opportunities.

The Disabilities Affinity Group – The Disabilities Affinity Group (DAG) was established to increase awareness of people with disabilities and their concerns. The group also educates its members on the options for accessibility here at the bank.

The group includes associates who have a disability and those who have a passion for the topic. Members share – and learn – options for care and services. The DAG has supported the bank's efforts during Disabilities Awareness Month, assisted with accessibility testing and worked on recruitment efforts. All of its activities line up with its mission to make Bank of America the most admired company for people with disabilities to bank, work and invest.

The Hispanic/Latino Organization for Leadership and Advancement (HOLA) – The Hispanic/Latino Organization for Leadership and Advancement (HOLA) is committed to helping Bank of America retain and develop its Hispanic/Latino associates. HOLA provides a forum through which its members can access the support and interest of senior managers in the bank. HOLA promotes inclusion and teamwork, helps associates learn more about the company, and engages associates and their families in enjoyable activities. Other opportunities include networking and the encouragement of self-initiated professional development.

LEAD for Women – LEAD (Leadership, Education, Advocacy, & Development) for Women is a network for women that concentrates on fostering their professional growth. It incorporates the missions undertaken in previous years by groups such as the Charlotte Women's Mentoring Group and the Women's Interest Network.

LEAD aims to help the bank hire, encourage and retain successful women. The group focuses on providing women with opportunities for leadership, advancement and expanding their horizons. A variety of methods, including the sharing of information, education, advocacy and networking, are used. The members of LEAD learn best work practices from one another and cultivate connections that can foster their success.

The Parents Affinity Group – The Parents Affinity Group draws on the knowledge and experience of its primary members – working parents – and uses these resources to make their work/life better. The Parents Group endeavors to determine the concerns of its members and develops tactics that will enable a more positive experience for those who balance work and family life. The group has employed newsletters, seminars, networking lists, recognition events and brochures to accomplish its mission of cultivating an environment that recognizes parents' issues. The group seeks to increase awareness of options for the mutual benefit of its members, their managers and the corporation.

Entry-level Programs/Full-time Opportunities/Training Programs

Banc of America Securities (BAS) offers full-time opportunities in: Corporate & Investment Banking; Capital Markets; Global Markets – Sales & Trading; Research; and Global Portfolio Management. All analysts begin their career at BAS with an extensive training program in New York City, our main base of operation. The first part of the program combines analysts from all lines of business within Global Capital Markets & Investment Banking (GCIB) and is designed to provide everyone with common foundational skills in accounting and corporate finance and a working knowledge of the products and businesses of the bank. Following the first two weeks, analysts participate in a program specifically designed to prepare them for their new roles.

The full program is a combination of classroom instruction, e-learning modules, case studies, presentations and trading simulations. Throughout the program, analysts have ample opportunities to work closely with professionals and peers throughout our organization including professionals in investment banking, capital markets, sales, trading, research and portfolio/risk management. This is a great opportunity to build a network of colleagues across the firm and will prove to be a tremendous resource.

In their new jobs, analysts will have access to ongoing education to help them achieve expertise in their specific business area. Our Learning and Organizational Effectiveness (LOE) team recently launched the GCIB Learning Network, which is a repository of information on all the development opportunities available at Banc of

America Securities. By accessing the system analysts can enroll in and view all course objectives, logistics and pre-work assigned to the e-learning modules and programs that have been developed for the entry-level population. Analysts will be directed to learning paths that will help them optimize the specific learning opportunities available to enhance their career.

For more information on our full-time analyst programs, please visit bofa.com/careers.

Diversity Mission Statement

The Bank of America Core Values
The following five values represent what we believe in as individuals and as a team, and how we aspire to interact with our customers, our shareholders, our communities and one another.

Inclusive Meritocracy
We care about one another, focus on results and strive to help all associates reach their full potential. We respect and value our differences.

Doing the right thing
We have the responsibility to do the right thing for our customers, shareholders, communities and one another.

Trusting & Teamwork
We rely on one another and succeed together. We take collective responsibility for the quality of our customers' experiences.

Winning
We have a passion for achieving results and winning – for our customers, our shareholders, our communities and our teammates.

Leadership
We will be decisive leaders at every level, communicating our vision and taking action to help build a better future.

Additional Information

At Bank of America, we are committed to an "inclusive meritocracy" – a work environment where all associates are welcomed, included and rewarded for good work. We respect and value not only differences of race, gender, ethnicity and sexual orientation, but also diversity of viewpoint, experience, talents and ideas. We work to empower all associates to excel on the job and to reach their full potential, and we reward and recognize associates based on performance and results.

Encouraging a diverse, inclusive workplace gives us the business advantage of understanding and satisfying the needs of our diverse customers, business clients and shareholders. Our diversity also provides fresh ideas and perspectives, which promotes ingenuity.

Bank of America addresses diversity and inclusion on a wide variety of fronts:

In recruiting new associates to join our company, including maintaining long-term partnerships with diverse national professional associations to help in our recruiting efforts

- In professional development for the associates who are already on our team

- In our Supplier Diversity & Development purchasing programs to support the growth of minority-, disabled- and woman-owned businesses in America, which is the largest of its kind among Fortune 500 companies and has received more than 70 awards

- In our targeted customer group marketing designed to meet the diverse demographic and ethnic groups we serve in a manner that is relevant and speci?c to their needs

- In our support of our communities, including local Team Bank of America Networks and $2 million in scholarship pledges to the United Negro College Fund, Hispanic Scholarship Fund and Native American Scholarship Fund

Because we serve such a diverse population, diversity is more than the right thing for Bank of America to do – it's a business imperative.

Barclays Capital

Barclays Capital
200 ParK Avenue
New York, NY 10166
Phone: 212-412-4000
Fax: 212-412-6795
www.barclayscapital.com/campusrecruitment/

Locations

Barclays Capital is headquartered in London and has offices in:

Europe, the Middle East and Africa:
Amsterdam • Birmingham • Dubai • Frankfurt • Geneva • Johannesburg • Lugano • Madrid • Manchester • Milan • Paris • Reading • Zurich

The Americas:
Boston • Chicago • Los Angeles • Mexico City • Miami • New York • San Francisco • Sao Paulo • Washington • Whippany

Asia Pacific:
Bangkok • Beijing • Hong Kong • Jakarta • Kuala Lumpur • Labuan • Mumbai • Seoul • Shanghai • Singapore • Sydney • Tokyo

Contact Information

Contact Person: Christina DelliSanti-Miller, Head of Diversity, Americas
Diversity Manager: Jacqueline Gibbs
Diversity Campus Recruiting Team Leader: Tara Udut - Head of Campus Recruiting, Americas

Strategic Plan and Diversity Leadership

How does the firm's leadership communicate the importance of diversity to everyone at the firm?

Tom Kalaris is the senior executive charged with representing the firm's Diversity agenda. As CEO of the Americas, and a member of the firm's Executive Committee, Tom is the primary communicator of our commitment to diversity.

It is his and Michael Evans', Global Head of HR (see below), responsibility to ensure that diversity and what it means is part of everyday business at the firm.

The importance of diversity is further communicated through our Diversity Committee, Employee Forums and sponsorships. Employees can access information via the diversity web site, emails and monthly diversity and employee forum group meetings.

Who has primary responsibility for leading overall diversity initiatives at your firm?

Michael Evans as the Global Head of Human Resources leads the primary business group responsible for supporting and facilitating all the efforts of the individuals in diversity initiatives throughout the firm.

Who has primary responsibility for diversity recruiting initiatives at your firm, if different from above?

Tara Udut, as Head of Campus Recruiting, Americas: Tara and her group work with regional campus recruiting committees as well as targeted campus teams to ensure that Diversity is an important business consideration. Each team has an executive charged with ensuring specific focus on diverse student representation.

Pamela Sinclair, Director, HR - Front Office and Janice Von Bulow, Director, HR - Infrastructure: As heads of our Client Relationship Teams, they have responsibility for ensuring that Diversity related recruiting initiatives are integrated in the experienced hire arena. They regularly reinforce our commitment to Diversity with our search partners and review how their performance contributes to furthering our Diversity agenda.

Does your firm currently have a diversity committee? Yes

If yes, does the committee's representation include one or more members of the firm's management/executive committee (or the equivalent)?

Yes, the committee consists of senior representation from all areas of the firm.

If yes, how many senior managers are on the committee, and how often did the committee convene in furtherance of the firm's diversity initiatives in 2004?

Total senior managers on committee: 8
Number of diversity meetings annually: 12, once a month

Does the committee(s) and/or diversity leader establish and set goals or objectives consistent with management's priorities?

Yes, we use a model that focuses our initiatives along three key work streams- recruit, develop and retain, with a designated senior manager responsible for progress along each stream.

Has the firm undertaken a formal or informal diversity program or set of initiatives aimed at increasing the diversity of the firm?

Yes, formal - to reiterate, a broad range of staff are committed to initiatives within each of three major work streams.

How often does the firm's management review the firm's diversity progress/results? Monthly

Are the members of the diversity committee or committees involved in diversity activities?

Yes. Our management team is active in ensuring that Diversity is integrated into the way we do business on a daily basis (i.e., people, policies and practices).

Diversity Council members take a leadership/champion role in Diversity initiatives (e.g. recruitment, development, etc) and Networking Group activity.

Tom Kalaris makes Diversity a regular topic at all-employee meetings. Senior management meetings throughout the year periodically include reinforcement of our Diversity commitment.

Recruitment of New Analysts and Associates

On-campus

Does your firm annually recruit at any of the following types of institutions?

- Ivy League schools
- Public state schools
- Private schools
- Historically Black Colleges and Universities (HBCUs)
- Hispanic Serving Institutions (HSIs)
- Other predominantly minority and/or women's colleges
- Active partners with Sponsors for Educational Opportunity Program and Inroads

Of the schools that you listed above, do you have any special outreach efforts directed to encourage minority students to consider your firm?

- Hold a reception for minority students
- Conferences
- Advertise in minority student association publication(s)
- Participate in/host minority student job fair(s)
- Sponsor minority student association events
- Firm's professionals participate on career panels at school
- Outreach to leadership of minority student organizations
- Scholarships or intern/fellowships for minority students
- Contest/Challenge
- Outreach to sororities, fraternities and other minority student clubs
- Conducted first ever Trading Challenge at Howard University

Professional Recruiting

What activities does the firm undertake to attract women and minorities?

- Partner programs with women and minority banking associations
- Conferences
- Participate at minority job fairs
- Seek referrals from other professionals
- Utilize online job services

Do you use executive recruiting/search firms to seek to identify new diversity hires? Yes

Affinity Groups/Employee Networks

We have four active employee forums in the Americas and one in the U.K., with several others being formed in the U.K.

Americas:

Barclays Cultural Alliance - Ethnicity networking group
GLBT Network - Gay and Lesbian networking group
Women's Leadership Forum - Women's networking group
Disability Champions Network - Disability networking group

U.K.:

Women's Internal Network - Women's networking group

Purpose: Employee Forums are open to all employees and are recognized by the firm for their support of business and diversity goals

Diversity Mission Statement

At Barclays Capital we are committed to providing creative and innovative solutions for our clients and the attraction and retention of world-class professionals enables us to fulfill that commitment. We actively promote Diversity to sustain continued business success and therefore we:

Seek to build a workforce that reflects the communities in which we live and work so that we are best able to meet the needs of our clients.

Strive to ensure that the talents of all our employees are fully utilized and that no job applicant or employee will receive less favorable treatment on the grounds of race, religion, gender, age, physical ability, sexual orientation, or nationality.

Aim to provide our employees with a working environment which encourages dignity and respect and is free from discrimination and harassment.

Aspire to be an employer that has a reputation for fairness, integrity, innovation, and creativity in order to attract and retain clients as well as potential and existing employees.

Diversity is a business imperative and we are committed to being an organization that values Diversity and promotes the inclusion of all people who share the firm's aspirations and performance expectations.

Additional Information

Barclays Capital supports the National Black MBA Association, the National Society of Hispanic MBAs, Sponsors for Educational Opportunity, and Inroads

The National Black MBA is a business organization that leads in the creation of economic and intellectual wealth fro the African-American community. One of the main operating principals of the NBMBA is to establish and maintain an effective nationwide information and communication network. Additionally, the NBMBA enhances the membership's professional and career development goals that link Black business professionals.

The National Society of Hispanic MBA's fosters Hispanic leadership through graduate management education and professional development. NSHMBA is dedicated to increasing the enrollment of Hispanics in Graduate Management. Its program assists corporations in the recruitment, development and promotion of Hispanic business professionals and provides networking opportunities.

Inroads is a program whose mission to develop and place talented students of color in business and industry to prepare them for corporate and community leadership

Sponsors for Educational Opportunity is a program that places outstanding college students of color in substantive internships that are designed to lead to full-time jobs with Wall Street firms.

Bear, Stearns & Co., Inc.

383 Madison Avenue
New York, NY 10179
(212) 272-2000
www.bear.com

Locations

19 locations worldwide

Departments

Asset Management
Custodial Trust
Derivatives
Equities
Fixed Income
Global Clearing Services
Investment Banking
Merchant Banking
Private Client Services

The Stats

Revenue (2004): $6,812.9 million
Chairman & CEO: James E. Cayne
Employer Type: Public company

Contact Information

Resumes can be submitted online at the careers section of www.bearstearns.com

E-mail:
hresources_internet@bear.com

Diversity URL:
www.bearstearns.com/bear/bsportal/Info.do?left=About%20Bear%20Stearns&top=Diversity

Recruitment of New Analysts and Associates

Do you have any special outreach efforts directed to encourage minority students to consider your firm?

Bear Stearns attends the following:

- Whitney M. Young Jr. Memorial Conference (Wharton) and Career Fair
- AMBLE Wall Street Luncheon (Harvard)
- Columbia Black Business Students Association Conference and Career Fair
- NYU – Association of Hispanic and Black Business Students Conference and Career Fair
- University of Chicago Annual DuSable Business Conference
- Robert F. Toigo Apex Orientation
- Consortium for Graduate Study in Management
- National Black MBA Association
- National Society of Hispanic MBAs
- National Association of Black Accountants
- Association of Latino Professionals in Finance & Accounting
- Asian Diversity Career Fair
- Urban Financial Services Coalition
- Department of Labor Hispanic Job Fair
- NAACP Job Fair

What activities does the firm undertake to attract women and minorities?

- Partner programs with women and minority banking associations
- Diversity Wall Street Event
- SEC Committee on Equal Opportunity Career Fair

Partner Organizations

Consortium for Graduate Study in Management

The Consortium for Graduate Study in Management is a nonprofit group of fourteen graduate business schools dedicated to providing management education opportunities to under-represented minorities seeking business careers. With support from American corporations and foundations, the Consortium provides merit-based full-tuition scholarships and fees to enable its Fellows to enroll in graduate business programs. The fourteen member universities are dedicated to challenging and improving their students' analytical, problem-solving and decision-making abilities crucial to professional managerial success. Today there are more than 4,000 alumni of the Consortium Fellowship Program.

The Robert Toigo Foundation
The Robert Toigo foundation is a Financial Services Fellowship program which provides fellowships to minority students attending some of the country's most prestigious graduate schools. In addition to financial support, the foundation offers mentorship and leadership training to their Fellows.

The National Society of Hispanic MBAs
The NSHMBA was launched in 1989 and fosters Hispanic leadership through graduate management education and professional development. The Society is dedicated to increasing the enrollment of Hispanics in Graduate Management. The NSHMBA program assists corporations in the recruitment, development and promotion of Hispanic business professionals and provides networking opportunities.

National Black MBA Association
The National Black MBA Association, Inc., (NBMBAA), is a business organization that leads in the creation of economic and intellectual wealth for the African-American community. One of the main operating principals of the NBMBA is to establish and maintain an effective nationwide information and communication network. Additionally, the NBMBAA enhances the membership's professional and career development goals that link black business professionals.

Financial Women's Association
The Financial Women's Association (FWA) advances professionalism in the field of finance, with special emphasis on the role of women and the development of future leaders. Founded in 1956, FWA is a leading executive organization of over 1,200 members committed to shaping leaders in business and finance. The FWA serves its members through educational programs and networking opportunities, and serves the community through its nationally acclaimed scholarship, mentoring and training programs.

Additional Information

Commitment to Diversity within a Meritocracy
Bear Stearns is a world-class financial institution with a relentless drive to succeed and an understanding that our employees are the key to our success. A major

component of our continued growth and vitality is our ability to attract and retain the best talent in the marketplace regardless of physical or cultural differences. We are committed to remaining a meritocracy where talent, intelligence and diligence are recognized, individual efforts are supported and employees are respected for their unique qualities. Our workforce represents the diverse multiethnic, multicultural nature of the societies in which we do business and extends beyond the limitations of race, sex, religion, age, national origin, disability or sexual orientation.

In pursuit of recruiting the best people at both entry and experienced levels, we have established a number of efforts including partnering with organizations that assist minority students and women and foster their career development. To this end, we participate in numerous outreach events throughout the year so that we may meet exceptional talent and encourage them to apply for positions at Bear Stearns. We are also directly involved with a number of first-rate organizations to connect with a breadth of minority communities.

Another cornerstone of our pledge to diversity is a dedication to mentoring programs for everyone – from young professionals developing to their full potential to senior staff seeking career assistance. Many Bear Stearns employees have mentored inner-city children through the Bear Stearns Partners in Education program. We established the BearCares Mentoring program in conjunction with Tuesday's Children and the National Mentoring Partnership to match employees for one year with children and teens who lost a parent or caregiver in the Sept. 11th disaster. In addition, we are proud to have developed a number of programs to accommodate our employees' busy schedules including the Everybody Wins Power Lunch literacy program and weekends with Big Brothers/Big Sisters of NYC exposing at-risk children to educational, vocational and cultural opportunities.

Brown Brothers Harriman & Co.

140 Broadway
New York, NY 10005
Phone: 212-493-8945
Fax: 212-493-7287
www.bbh.com

Locations

New York, NY (HQ)
Boston, MD
Charlotte, NC
Chicago, IL
Dallas, TX
Jersey City, NJ
Los Angeles, CA
Palm Beach, FL
Philadelphia, PA

Dublin
Grand Cayman
London
Luxembourg
Hong Kong
Tokyo
Zurich

Contact Information

Contact Person: Laura Spong, Director of Recruiting
Diversity Team Leader/Diversity Campus Recruiting Team Leader: Jim Minogue, Head of Human Resources

Strategic Plan and Diversity Leadership

How does the firm's leadership communicate the importance of diversity to everyone at the firm?
BBH's employee handbook outlines very clearly BBH's commitment to diversity and equal employment opportunities. In addition, BBH's commitment to diversity is constantly reinforced throughout the entire recruitment process – from stressing our diversity efforts to external vendors, to conveying the importance to hiring managers.

Who has primary responsibility for leading overall diversity initiatives at your firm?
Jim Minogue, Head of Human Resources

Who has primary responsibility for diversity recruiting initiatives at your firm, if different from?
Laura Spong, Director of Recruiting

Does your firm currently have a diversity committee? No

Does the committee(s) and/or diversity leader establish and set goals or objectives consistent with management's priorities? Yes

Has the firm undertaken a formal or informal diversity program or set of initiatives aimed at increasing the diversity of the firm? Yes, informal

How often does the firm's management review the firm's diversity progress/results? Annually

How are the firm's diversity committee(s) and/or firm management held accountable for achieving results?
There are annual reviews of promotions and compensation recommendations in which management reviews the progress of minorities and women within BBH. Senior managers challenge direct line managers to review when statistics do not show progress.

Recruitment of New Analysts and Associates

On-campus

Please list the schools at which your school recruits.

- *Public state schools:* Rutgers University, Baruch College
- *Private schools:* Boston University, Pace University, Connecticut College, Trinity College, Northeastern University, Bryant College, Holy Cross College, Boston College

Of the schools that you listed above, do you have any special outreach efforts directed to encourage minority students to consider your firm? No

Professional Recruiting

What activities does the firm undertake to attract women and minorities? Minority job fairs as well as reinforcing the commitment to diversity with vendors when we sign contracts and begin searches

Do you use executive recruiting/search firms to seek to identify new diversity hires? Yes

Internships

Brown Brothers Harriman does not, at this time, have a formal internship program.

Entry-level Programs/Full-time Opportunities/Training Programs

Corporate Banking & Management Development Program

Length of program: 18 weeks
Geographic location(s) of program: New York

Please describe the training/training component of this program:
Corporate Banking Analysts will attend our 18-week Management Development Program, after which they will join one of the regional or product specialty groups within the Corporate Banking group, under the leadership of a Senior Relationship Manager.

Initial responsibilities will include:

- Financial analysis in support of new business initiatives
- Credit analysis, including preparation of financial spreadsheets and written credit reports
- Client relations support

As their experience develops over time, analysts are expected to take on relationship management and business development responsibilities.

The Management Development Program

The Brown Brothers Harriman Management Development Program is an 18-week intensive program for new undergraduate hires in Corporate Banking, Investment Management, Investor Services and Treasury. The program includes class instruction, case studies and presentations by BBH business leaders. Classes are conducted by instructors from top business schools. Subjects include Financial Accounting (Introduction and Advanced), Money & Banking and Corporate Finance. All participants are joined with a mentor to give additional guidance and professional insight.

Institutional Services Training Program

Length of program: 1-2 weeks
Geographic location(s) of program: New Jersey/Boston

Please describe the training/training component of this program:
3 weeks of training to include product training, as well as BBH-specific training.

Please describe any other educational components of this program: Tuition reimbursement, on-the-job training and additional internal training classes

Additional Information

EEO Statement

The success of any business depends upon the caliber of its employees. Brown Brothers Harriman has long prided itself on employing and retaining an unusually competent, loyal and well-qualified staff. The firm employs men and women on the basis of their abilities, experience and aptitudes. Brown Brothers Harriman is committed to the principles of affirmative action and to compliance with all federal, state and local laws concerning employment discrimination. To this end, it is the policy of Brown Brothers Harriman to offer equal opportunities and reasonable accommodation to all qualified employees and applicants for employment without regard to race, sex, veteran status, application for or service in the Armed Forces Reserve, citizenship status, disability, color, age, religion, creed, national origin, ancestry, marital status, handicap, atypical hereditary cellular blood trait, familial status, affectional or sexual orientation. This commitment includes, without limitation, the areas of hiring (or failing or refusing to hire), placement, transfer, promotion, treatment during employment, advertising, use of firm facilities, recreational activities, working conditions, layoff, termination, rates of pay, benefits, selection for training and any other company-related programs.

The reasons for this policy are many. It is good business to use all available human resources to meet present and future employment needs. We recognize that the business community has an obligation to take action toward solving the problems of our city. Most important of all, though, we hold a moral conviction that it is wrong to judge a person on factors which are not job related. While we have legal obligations to meet, we are engaged in this effort because we believe it is the right thing to do.

We should be clear that we are not talking about a passive policy of non-discrimination. We are, instead, engaged in an active effort to recruit, hire and promote qualified members of minority groups and females.

Employees with disabilities that may require reasonable accommodation to allow them to perform their jobs are responsible for bringing this request to the attention of their department head. Department heads should then notify the Director of Human Resources, who is responsible for determining reasonable accommodation.

The partners have every intention of making equal opportunity a reality at BBH. We count upon all of our associates to do their part in making it work. Responsibility for insuring compliance with the firm's Equal Employment Opportunity Policy Statement has been given to the Director of Human Resources. This policy, while a continuing one, will be updated and reviewed from time to time at intervals no longer than annually.

BBH Affirmative Action Statement

It has been and will continue to be the policy and practice of the firm and its officers to ensure equal employment opportunities without regard to race, sex, disabled veteran or Vietnam-era veteran status, application for or service in the Armed Forces Reserve, citizenship status, disability, color, age, religion, creed, national origin, ancestry, marital status, handicap, atypical hereditary cellular blood trait, familial status, affectional or sexual orientation, and to affirmatively seek to ensure that there is equality of opportunity in all terms and conditions of employment. The Partners expect all officers and employees to accept and to reflect the spirit of these principles in their daily working relationships.

The above-stated policy and the Affirmative Action Plan ("AAP") confirm the firm's commitment to:

- Recruit, hire, train and promote in accordance with the principles of equal employment opportunity

- Ensure that promotion decisions comply with the principles of equal employment opportunity

- Ensure that all personnel actions, including compensation, benefits, transfers, terminations, company sponsored training, tuition assistance and social and recreational programs are administered in accordance with the principles of equal opportunity

- Reaffirm its policy to provide equal employment opportunities to qualified handicapped persons, disabled veterans and Vietnam-era veterans.

James J. Minogue, Director of Human Resources, has been appointed the Equal Opportunity Officer for Brown Brothers Harriman & Co. and has the overall responsibility for implementing, monitoring and communicating the firm's policy.

Work/Life Balance

Brown Brothers Harriman has thrived for almost 200 years on the strength of its people. Our employee's innovative ideas, commitment to quality and excellent and focus on client service have all contributed to the success of the firm.

Attracting the best people and providing them with a supportive environment in which they can grow, develop and contribute to the firm's success in a meaningful way has been and will continue to be a primary focus of the firm. This supportive environment is, in part, achieved by our offering a suite of benefits, programs and resources to our employees. Whether our employees are working to balance their work and personal life, are looking for a way to give back to the community, are seeking information about elder care services, or are looking for ways to save money through payroll deductions or profit sharing plans, BBH offers the resources to help.

Achieving our mission is accomplished through our people. We believe that our people deserve a premier environment in which to work with the appropriate benefits, programs and resources. We intend to support our employees and their changing needs for years to come.

Flexible Work Arrangements Guiding Principles

We value our employees, and our support of FWAs reflects our trust in them. We seek to be an Employer of Choice, attracting the best people and retaining employees who are committed to the firm. We recognize that there are differences among BBH employees and encourage creativity and initiative in addressing employee needs while simultaneously meeting or exceeding client expectations.

Excellent client service is critical to our continued success. At BBH, we are committed to achieving excellence and consider Flexible Work Arrangements to be part of our business strategy that supports superior client service. FWAs need to fit with our business priorities and the nature of the job.

FWAs support the individuality of BBH employees without compromising teamwork, collaboration and mutual flexibility. Ongoing communication and collaboration of employees, managers and work groups is critical in all aspects of our business, including the effective implementation of FWAs. A mutual give and take occurs as needed, without taking advantage of an employee's or a manager's willingness to make periodic schedule adjustments in accessibility.

CIBC World Markets

300 Madison Avenue
New York, NY 10017
Phone: 212-856-4000
Email: employment@us.cibc.com
www.cibcwm.com

Locations

New York, NY (U.S. HQ)
Atlanta, GA
Baltimore, MD
Boston, MD
Chicago, IL
Denver, CO
Houston, TX
Los Angeles, CA
Menlo Park, CA
St. Louis, MO
Salt Lake City, VT
San Francisco, CA
Seattle, WA

Toronto (World HQ)
Beijing
Calgary
Dublin
Hong Kong
London
Montreal
Ottawa
Singapore
Sydney
Tel Aviv
Tokyo
Vancouver

The Stats

Revenue (2004): $2.85 billion (worldwide)

Diversity Mission Statement

CIBC's global commitment to workplace equity and diversity is reflected in the following principles:

Employment decisions are based on merit. Capabilities, attributes and individual performance are the key criteria for hiring and promotion.

The value placed on the diversity of our workforce, where differences such as gender, racial or ethnic origin, age, religious belief or disability present no barriers to individual opportunity.

Providing a work environment that is inclusive and non-discriminatory, and establishing effective mechanisms for responding to the individual needs of employees and job candidates.

Striving toward achieving accessibility to CIBC's systems and physical workplaces.

Meeting local regulatory requirements in all jurisdictions where we do business.

CIBC's global policies further reflect this commitment. These include: Global Hiring and Global Workplace Accommodation policies, and the Global Policy and Guidelines/Procedures on Harassment in the Workplace.

Additional Information

In the U.S., CIBC's specific regional policy regarding employment and the workplace is laid out in the following Equal Employment Opportunity policy.

CIBC USA is committed to a policy of recruiting and employing the individuals who are best qualified to perform the duties of each position regardless of age, race, creed, color, national origin, sexual orientation, military status, sex, disability, genetic predisposition or carrier status, marital status, citizenship or any other legally protected condition. All employees are treated in a non-discriminatory manner with respect to all terms and conditions of employment. In addition, CIBC USA is committed to providing a work environment that is free from sexual harassment. All employees are expected to comply with and reinforce these principles when carrying out their day to day responsibilities.

Citigroup

388 Greenwich St, 20th Fl
New York, NY 10013
Phone: 212-816-2790
Fax: 212-816-5118
www.citigroup.com

Locations

Asia, Australia, Europe, Japan, Latin America and North America

The Stats

Revenue (2004): $21.8 billion (worldwide)

Contact Information

Contact Person: Patricia David Managing Director, Global Diversity

Diversity Team Leader/Diversity Campus Recruiting Team Leader: Danielle Orkin, Vice President, CIB Campus Recruiting
e-mail: danielle.f.orkin@citigroup.com

Diversity URL:
www.citigroup.com/citigroup/citizen/diversity/index.htm

Strategic Plan and Diversity Leadership

How does the firm's leadership communicate the importance of diversity to everyone at the firm?

Citigroup Corporate and Investment Banking (CIB) regularly communicates the importance of diversity to everyone at our firm through a variety of communication vehicles, including but not limited to:

- E-mails
- Intranet web-sites
- Internal Employee Publications (e.g., Diversity Yearbook, annual Diversity Calendar)
- Employee Newsletters
- All-employee Meetings (i.e. town halls)

Who has primary responsibility for leading overall diversity initiatives at your firm?
Elizabeth Riccardelli
Vice President, Corporate Recruiting

Patricia David
Managing Director, Global Head of Diversity & Employee Programs, Citigroup Corporate and Investment Banking (CIB)

Who has primary responsibility for diversity recruiting initiatives at your firm, if different from?

Danielle F. Orkin
Vice President, Corporate & Investment Banking Campus Recruiting

Does your firm currently have a diversity committee? Yes

If yes, does the committee's representation include one or more members of the firm's management/executive committee (or the equivalent)? Yes

If yes, how many senior managers are on the committee, and how often did the committee convene in furtherance of the firm's diversity initiatives in 2004?
All members of the CIB's senior management team are on diversity committees. The CIB Diversity Operating Committee, comprised of senior business and Human Resources leaders from our core businesses, support functions and global regions, meets on a monthly basis to review progress against the strategy, share best practices and align efforts globally where possible. CIB senior management also reviews overall efforts on a quarterly basis.

If you have more than one diversity committee, please list.
In the U.S., each core business and support function has a diversity committee in which business leadership and employees from various levels and functional groups develop and execute strategies and initiatives. Many have layered organizational structures with sub-committees tasked to deliver on specific efforts (e.g., communications, recruiting, career development, etc.). Outside of the U.S., each of our major regions has a cross-business diversity committee in place to develop and execute strategies and initiatives, and depending on the structure of diversity efforts in a particular region, there may be additional committees to drive specific efforts. Engaging business leadership and employees at all levels in making progress against our diversity strategy is a fundamental component of our organization.

Does the committee(s) and/or diversity leader establish and set goals or objectives consistent with management's priorities? Yes

Has the firm undertaken a formal or informal diversity program or set of initiatives aimed at increasing the diversity of the firm? Yes, formal

How often does the firm's management review the firm's diversity progress/results? Quarterly

How are the firm's diversity committee(s) and/or firm management held accountable for achieving results?
We are working to ensure that our business and support functions and their managers develop diversity plans and are increasingly held accountable for progress against those plans. The CIB's senior management team reviews overall efforts and results on a quarterly basis, and annual performance reviews for this group include a component on diversity. At the company level (i.e., Citigroup Inc.), senior management's overall efforts, which are linked to compensation, are reviewed every quarter with Citigroup's President and COO and are also reported to Citigroup's Board of Directors.

Are the members of the diversity committee or committees involved in diversity activities?
Yes. While the wide range of activities in which committee members get involved are far too numerous to list, a short representative sample includes:

> Targeted recruiting events, both on-campus and internally organized efforts, throughout the year
>
> Mentoring programs, including both one-on-one and one-to-many relationships. A great example is our "family sponsor" concept, popular in many of our

divisions, in which senior managers typically are assigned a group of targeted employees from various functional areas. The group meets regularly with the senior manager over a specified time period, and one-on-one meetings also take place, in an effort to foster exposure, networking and mentoring opportunities for the targeted group. As an example, CIB senior management team members (global business and support function heads) based in our NY headquarters were assigned a group of 8-10 employees with whom they met regularly over a nine month period.

Our networking initiatives are extensive and senior managers and diversity committee members have an excellent track record of personally attending these types of functions.

Training and Career Development programs are offered to many employees via our diversity committees' efforts and where possible senior management's participation, perhaps as advisors or mentors, is a core component of the program.

Sponsorship of external organizations whose efforts support our diversity strategy offers us many opportunities to attend external conferences, dinners, etc. or to contribute to the organization's development by assigning representatives to Corporate Advisory councils, to the organization's Board of Directors, etc. Our senior managers and diversity committee members have consistently demonstrated their support by becoming personally involved to help us build and benefit from our strategic partnerships.

Recruitment of New Analysts and Associates

On-campus

Please list the schools at which your firm recruits.

- *Ivy League schools:* Brown, Columbia, Cornell, Dartmouth, Harvard, University of Pennsylvania, Princeton and Yale

- *Public state schools:* Berkeley, University of Maryland, University of Michigan, Texas A&M, University of Illinois, University of Texas, University of Toronto, UCLA, USC, UVA, Baruch, New Jersey Institute of Technology, SUNY-Stonybrook, Rutgers, University of Florida and University of North Carolina.

- *Private schools:* Claremont McKenna, Duke, Georgetown, Emory, Amherst, Holy Cross, Notre Dame, NYU, Stanford, University of Miami, University of Western Ontario, Boston University, Farleigh Dickinson, Hofstra, Northwestern, St. John's University, Stevens Institute, Babson, University of Colorado, Carnegie Mellon, Fordham, Johns Hopkins University, Lafayette, McGill, Middlebury, MIT, Minnesota, Northwestern, Pace, Rice, Richmond, Vanderbilt, Williams and Washington University-St. Louis.

- *Historically Black Colleges and Universities (HBCUs):* Morehouse, Howard, Spelman, Clark Atlanta and Florida A&M

- *Women's colleges:* Barnard, Smith

Of the schools that you listed above, do you have any special outreach efforts directed to encourage minority students to consider your firm?

- Hold a reception for minority students
- Conferences
- Advertise in minority student association publication(s)
- Participate in/host minority student job fair(s)
- Sponsor minority student association events
- Firm's professionals participate on career panels at school
- Outreach to leadership of minority student organizations
- Scholarships or intern/fellowships for minority students

Professional Recruiting

What activities does the firm undertake to attract women and minorities?

- Partner programs with women and minority banking associations (e.g. Women of Color)
- Conferences: Rainbow Push, Reaching Out, NBMBA and NSHMBA
- Participate at minority job fairs
- Seek referrals from other professionals
- Utilize online job services

Do you use executive recruiting/search firms to seek to identify new diversity hires? Yes

Internships

Summer Analyst Program

Deadline for application for the internship: March 2006
Number of interns in the program in summer 2004: 152
Pay ($US): 2,292.00 (pre-tax) bi-monthly
Length of the program: 10 weeks
Program Web site: www.citigroup.com/citigroup/careers/homepage/

Citigroup's Corporate and Investment Bank offers a 10-week internship in the following departments:

- **Global Banking** – Global Portfolio Management, Global Relationship Bank and Investment Banking

- **Global Transaction Services**

- **Corporate Infrastructure** – Finance, Operations and Technology

- **Capital Markets** – Sales & Trading, Public Finance, Quantitative Trading & Research, Structured Corporate Finance and Capital Markets

Responsibilities and admission vary by division.

Candidates who meet the following criteria will be considered for the Summer Analyst program:

- You are currently a junior pursuing a Baccalaureate Degree

- You have maintained a minimum cumulative GPA of 3.5

- You are a U.S. citizen, lawful U.S. permanent resident or foreign national authorized to work in the U.S., provided that Citigroup will not be required to sponsor you to extend or maintain your work authorization. (This program is not open to any foreign national in the U.S. in F, J, M, Dependent E or L-2 nonimmigrant status.)

Scholarships

Investment Banking Global Diversity Scholarship Program

Deadline for application for the scholarship program: January 2006
Scholarship award amount: up to $10,000
Program web site or other contact information for scholarship:

Danielle Orkin
Vice President
388 Greenwich St, 20th Fl
New York, NY 10013
(212) 816-2790
danielle.f.orkin@citigroup.com

Our Scholarship Program was initially established to increase female and minority student interest in Citigroup and has now been broadened to expand the company's pool of prospective employees to include those individuals from all backgrounds who possess unique experiences. Students will be selected for the program on a competitive basis and we are looking for students who have demonstrated extraordinary performance as leaders on their campus as well as in their communities. Students who are juniors pursuing a Baccalaureate Degree will be considered for the program.

Each scholarship recipient will be granted a paid 10-week internship opportunity during the summer before their senior year and is eligible to receive a one-time award of up to $10,000, which will be granted upon successful completion of the summer internship.

In the selection process, we look for a number of the same qualities in our scholarship recipients that we consider essential for a successful career in Investment Banking. We search for a combination of academic and leadership excellence coupled with experiences and personal qualities that indicate an individual's potential to thoroughly benefit from the program and excel in the field of Investment Banking. Recipients of this scholarship are chosen from a group of finalists who are selected through a rigorous selection process. Students of all disciplines and majors are encouraged to apply. Please note that students who have not maintained a minimum cumulative GPA of 3.5 will not be considered for the program.

Affinity Groups/Employee Networks

African Heritage Network

The Citigroup African Heritage Network-NYC is an organization that seeks to support Citigroup's efforts to promote diversity in the organization by:

- Providing a forum for Citigroup employees to network and enhance their professional development

- Working with Citigroup's management to support their efforts in recruiting, developing and retaining top diverse talent

- Offering employees an opportunity to participate in community outreach projects

- Promoting education and awareness for all employees on issues that affect people of African heritage

Our goals are to:

- Develop a mentoring system for members

- Partner with Citigroup businesses to identify more focused training opportunities

For our members:

- Provide a venue for employee networking across businesses

- Partner with College Relations to assist with recruiting a diverse workforce

- Partner with professional organizations focused on the African heritage community to assist Citigroup with recruiting a diverse workforce

- Partner with Citigroup Community Relations on projects and initiatives that impact African heritage communities

- Build partnership with other employee networks

Asian Heritage Network

The Citigroup Asian Pacific Heritage Network is an organization that seeks to support Citigroup's efforts to promote diversity in the workplace by:

- Increasing awareness and sensitivity about Asian and Pacific Islander issues

- Increasing Citigroup's presence and contribution to the Asian and Pacific Islander communities in the NYC area

- Fostering a better understanding of the Asian and Pacific Islander cultures, including those of East, Central, South and South East Asia and the Pacific Islands

Hispanic Heritage Network

Citigroup Hispanic Network is an employee network that seeks to support Citigroup efforts to promote diversity in the organization by focusing on the following areas:

- Providing a forum for Citigroup employees with interest in Hispanic/Latin issues to network and enhance their professional development

- Working with Citigroup management to support their efforts in recruiting, developing and retaining top Hispanic/Latin talent

- Offering Citigroup employees an opportunity to participate in community outreach and social projects within the Hispanic/Latin community

- Promoting education and awareness for all Citigroup employees on issues related to Hispanics/Latins

There are other groups in the U.S. and Europe, including but not limited to supporting working parents, women, and Lesbian/Gay/Bisexual and Transgender (LGBT) employees.

Entry-level Programs/Full-time Opportunities/Training Programs

Finance Analyst Program

Length of program: 2 years
Geographic location(s) of program: New York

Please describe the training/training component of this program.

- All new Financial Analysts participate

- Classes are taught by a combination of Citigroup professionals and public accounting and business school professionals

- 4-5 week training program in New York: 2 weeks accounting, 1 week Finance; 1-2 weeks overview of Citigroup, CIB and Financial Division

- Accounting, finance and general business concepts taught

- Computer training: financial modeling utilizing Excel and word processing

- Financial Analysis: comparative and pro forma analysis

- Information sourcing: effectively using the firm's resources and outside databases.

- Each analyst is assigned a junior and senior mentor

Investment Banking Analyst Program

Length of program: 2 years
Geographic location(s) of program: Chicago, Dallas, Houston, Los Angeles, New York, San Francisco & Toronto

Please describe the training/training component of this program.
Training begins in mid-July in New York with five weeks of intensive classroom training, led by senior banking professionals in the firm as well as by outside advisors. The training program will cover:

- An overview of the investment banking business
- Accounting, finance and corporate finance
- Computer and information resources
- Financial modeling

In addition to classroom training, a number of social events are organized to allow networking between analysts in the program and senior banking professionals. All analysts are also assigned both a junior and senior mentor.

Global Corporate Finance Analyst Program

Length of program: 2 years
Geographic location(s) of program: New York

Please describe the training/training component of this program.
The Analyst Training program is approximately ten weeks in duration and provides the specific skills and knowledge needed to succeed at Citigroup. This program offers classes in financial accounting, corporate finance, analytics, cash flow modeling, risk and credit analysis and capital markets. Additionally, the training provides an understanding of the industry groups with whom you will work. Classes are taught by a combination of world-class consultants, university professors and banking professionals. Additionally, all analysts are assigned senior and junior mentors.

IT Analyst Program

Length of program: 2 years
Geographic location(s) of program: New York, New Jersey & Boston

Please describe the training/training component of this program.
On a monthly basis you will have a full day of classroom training and product orientation conducted by in-house trainers with special presentations by technology executives. You will be provided with the skills that will enable you to be a success at Citigroup. A sampling of the topics you will cover in the monthly training includes:

- Orientation
- Writing for Results
- Time Management
- Introduction to Firm Resources & Services
- Understanding the Performance Review Process/Setting Career Objectives
- Economic Update/Networking
- Understanding Work Styles
- Introduction to Global Markets
- Microsoft Project Fundamentals
- Presentation Skills
- Influence Skills

In addition, your manager, in consultation with our in-house technology training and development managers, may develop a personalized technology education curriculum that will enable you to expand your current technology skill set. All analysts are assigned senior and junior mentors.

Sales & Trading Analyst Program

Length of program: 2 years
Geographic location(s) of program: New York, Chicago, Boston & San Francisco

Please describe the training/training component of this program.

Three weeks of orientation and classroom training, followed by analysts rotating through various products areas that are participating in the program. Additionally, all analysts are assigned senior and junior mentors.

Capital Markets Analyst Program

Length of program: 2 years
Geographic location(s) of program: New York

Please describe the training/training component of this program.
Analysts come to New York in July for an intensive introduction to Citigroup's global businesses. During the first weeks of the program, analysts study concepts in corporate finance, accounting and financial modeling along with analysts from our Investment Banking division. Our goal is to help analysts develop a network, introduce them to the firm's resources and teach them how to use those resources to serve our clients.

Subsequently, Capital Markets Analysts begin a two-week intensive training course that focuses on financial products, securities analytics, bond math, credit and the businesses that are housed within Capital Markets. Finally, we prepare Capital Markets Analysts for the securities industries licenses, NASD Series 7 and Series 63. Additionally, all analysts are assigned senior and junior mentors.

Public Finance Analyst Program

Length of program: 2 years

Geographic location(s) of program: Atlanta, Boston, Chicago, Dallas, Fort Lauderdale, Houston, Los Angeles, Miami, New York City, Orlando, Philadelphia, San Francisco, Seattle, Tampa and West Palm Beach

Please describe the training/training component of this program.
We have an eight-week training program conducted by public finance professionals, attorneys and industry experts. The program covers bond math, financial modeling, credit analysis, tax and legal issues. Projects and case studies involving actual transactions are assigned to give new analysts hands-on experience as well as the opportunity to work in teams.

Global Transaction Services Analyst Program

Length of program: 2 years

Geographic location(s) of program: New York

Please describe the training/training component of this program.
• The program offers an initial six-week "boot-camp" style training period where you will gain in-depth training in accounting, credit/risk and financial analysis.

• All analysts are assigned senior and junior mentors.

Operations Analyst Program

Length of program: 2 Years
Geographic location(s) of program: New York

Please describe the training/training component of this program.

On a monthly basis you will have a full day of classroom training and product orientation conducted by in-house trainers with special presentations by technology executives. You will be provided with the skills that will enable you to be a success in Citigroup. Additionally, all analysts are assigned senior and junior mentors. A sampling of the topics you will cover in the monthly training includes:

- Orientation
- Writing for Results
- Time Management
- Introduction to Firm Resources and Services
- Understanding the Performance Review Process/Setting Career Objectives
- Economic Update/Networking
- Understanding Work Styles
- Introduction to Global Markets
- Microsoft Project Fundamentals
- Presentation Skills
- Introduction to Equities
- Influence Skills

Diversity Mission Statement

Citigroup's diversity strategy is based on four components – to be the employer of choice, service provider of choice, business partner of choice and neighbor of choice.

Employer of choice

Citigroup values a work environment where diversity is embraced, where people are promoted on their merits, and where people treat each other with mutual respect and dignity. Around the world, we are committed to being a company where the best people want to work; where opportunities to develop are widely available; where innovation and an entrepreneurial spirit are valued; and where a healthy work/life balance is encouraged.

Service provider of choice

Citigroup strives to deliver products and services to our customers that reflect both our global reach and our deep local roots in every market where we operate. The diversity of our employees enables us to better understand our customers, while the breadth of our product offerings allows us to serve them better.

Business partner of choice

Citigroup works to create mutually beneficial business relationships with minorities, women, disabled veterans and people with disabilities. We recognize that working with a wide range of professionals, suppliers and consultants strengthens the communities we serve and creates value for our shareholders.

Neighbor of choice

Citigroup believes it has a responsibility to make a difference in the neighborhoods in which we live and work around the world. We reach out to and form partnerships with nonprofit organizations, civic groups, educational institutions and local governments representing the diverse nature of these communities.

Credit Suisse First Boston

11 Madison Avenue
New York, NY 10010
Phone: 212-538-2594
Fax: 212-538-2594
www.csfb.com

Contact Information

Contact Person: Tanji Dewberry, Assistant Vice President (also Diversity Campus Recruiting Team Leader)
e-mail: tanji.dewberry@csfb.com

Strategic Plan and Diversity Leadership

How does the firm's leadership communicate the importance of diversity to everyone at the firm?
CSFB utilizes a variety of communication methods to convey the importance of diversity including newsletters, marketing brochures, e-mail memorandums, meetings and a website on the company intranet.

Who has primary responsibility for leading overall diversity initiatives at your firm?
Angie Casciato, Global Head of Diversity and Inclusion

Who has primary responsibility for diversity recruiting initiatives at your firm, if different from?
Tanji Dewberry, Assistant Vice President – for campus recruiting

Does your firm currently have a diversity committee? Yes

If yes, does the committee's representation include one or more members of the firm's management/executive committee (or the equivalent)? Yes

If yes, how many senior managers are on the committee, and how often did the committee convene in furtherance of the firm's diversity initiatives in 2004?)

Total senior managers on committee: 26
Number of diversity meetings annually: 6

If you have more than one diversity committee, please list.

Each of the below divisions have a Diversity Advisory Committee:
Alternative Capital Division, Corporate Investment Banking Division, Equity, Fixed Income and Finance, Administration & Operation

Does the committee(s) and/or diversity leader establish and set goals or objectives consistent with management's priorities? Yes

Has the firm undertaken a formal or informal diversity program or set of initiatives aimed at increasing the diversity of the firm? Yes, formal

How often does the firm's management review the firm's diversity progress/results? Quarterly

Are the members of the diversity committee or committees involved in diversity activities? Yes, the members of the diversity committees participate in diversity events at the firm as well as recruiting efforts.

If so, list and describe some of those activities.
Employee Network events, diversity recruiting events

Recruitment of New Analysts and Associates

On-campus

Please list the schools at which your firm recruits.

- Ivy League schools
- Public state schools
- Private schools
- Historically Black colleges and universities (HBCUs)
- Hispanic Serving Institutions (HSIs)
- Other predominantly minority and/or women's colleges

Of the schools that you listed above, do you have any special outreach efforts directed to encourage minority students to consider your firm?

- Hold a reception for minority students
- Conferences
- Advertise in minority student association publication: National Association of Black Accountants newsletter, Howard School of Business newspaper
- Participate in/host minority student job fairs
- Sponsor minority student association events
- Firm's professionals participate on career panels at school
- Outreach to leadership of minority student organizations
- Scholarships or intern/fellowships for minority students

Professional Recruiting

What activities does the firm undertake to attract women and minorities?

- Partner programs with women and minority business associations
- Conferences
- Participate at minority job fairs
- Seek referrals from other professionals
- Utilize online job services
- Market jobs to alumni networks of educational nonprofits

Do you use executive recruiting/search firms to seek to identify new diversity hires? Yes

Internships

Web site for information on all internships: www.csfb.com/standout

Summer Analyst – Corporate Investment Banking

Deadline for application for the internship: December
Length of the program: 10 weeks

Our 10-week Summer Analyst Program for rising college seniors gives you outstanding exposure to business and the financial services industry.

Whether you're working alongside a full-time Analyst or staffed as the only Analyst on a deal team, our summer program gives you the tools you'll need to jump-start your career in finance and investment banking. Responsibilities may include analyzing companies using financial modeling and valuation techniques, examining the impact of a transaction on a client's capital structure and analyzing the consequences of a merger or acquisition.

Summer Analysts will be placed directly into an industry or product group – in 2004, 100% of summer analysts received their first or second choice of groups. As a summer program participant, you will have the opportunity to work on deals in your group, gaining hands-on experience and working on all aspects of advising and transacting business for our clients. Summer Analysts are formally reviewed at the mid and end points of the summer, and offers are made on the last day of the program, enabling you to return to school with a full-time position secured.

Summer Analyst opportunities are available in New York, Chicago, Houston, Toronto, Los Angeles, Palo Alto and San Francisco. Our U.S. regional breadth offers unique opportunities to execute transactions from conception to close, which differentiates CSFB from our competitors.

Training

You'll attend a brief company orientation and a 7-day training program and then start work in your group for the summer, receiving further training while on the job.

Your learning experience will continue through the summer speaker series, where you'll hear from senior employees across the divisions. In addition, you'll participate in networking events and firm-wide events that will help ensure that you are exposed to all the areas within the bank and understand the big picture of a global investment bank. You'll also enjoy interacting with the other Summer Analysts and full time employees at a variety of social events throughout the summer

To help you determine your strengths and plan your career, summer analysts are matched with junior and senior mentors within Investment Banking, who provide advice and guidance throughout the summer.

Summer Analyst – Sales & Trading, Fixed Income or Equity

Deadline for application for the internship: December
Length of the program: 10 weeks

Program structure

The CSFB Securities Division offers two separate, 10-week summer programs – one in Equity Sales and Trading and one in Fixed Income Sales and Trading. If chosen for a first-round interview, students will interview for BOTH the Equity sales and trading and the Fixed Income sales and trading programs – please only drop your resume once for these programs. Second round interviews are held separately and will be Equity specific or Fixed Income specific. This will be determined based on your first round interviews. In both programs, you'll spend one week in training, followed by three separate three-week rotations on either Fixed Income or Equity desks.

Sales Rotation – You'll spend three weeks working within one sales product area. In Equity, this rotation will give you the chance to work with the Coverage Sales, Portfolio Sales, International Sales, Convertible Sales or Derivative sales teams. In Fixed Income, you'll work with the Corporate, Structured Products, Interest Rates, Global Foreign Exchange, Emerging Markets, CDO Group or Derivatives sales teams.

Trading Rotation – You'll spend three weeks working within one trading product area. In Fixed Income, these groups include the Corporate, Structured Products, Interest Rates, Global Foreign Exchange, Emerging Markets or Interest Rate Products trading teams. In Equity, it will include the Cash Trading, Derivative Trading, Program Trading, International Sales Trading and Exchange Traded Funds teams.

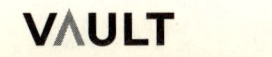

Sales or Trading Rotation – You'll spend your final three weeks on one of the above-mentioned sales or trading desks in either Fixed Income or Equity.

These programs are a great way to become familiar to the Sales and Trading arena, as well as the overall investment process, gaining a broad and varied view of several potential career paths.

Training and Content

Both programs provide summer analysts with the foundation necessary for a successful summer experience. They begin with an intense one-week training period in New York where all summer analysts participate in a capital markets overview, several desk overviews and a library tour. You'll be trained on Bloomberg and learn CSFB technology systems and databases. You'll tour the NYSE, and you'll meet with traders and salespeople from all of the various products.

After your first week of training, you'll hit the ground running, working to support a variety of desks within Fixed Income or Equity. Your learning experience will continue through the summer speaker series, where you'll hear from senior employees across the divisions. In addition, you'll participate in networking events, community service, and firm-wide events that will help ensure that you are exposed to all the areas within the bank and understand the big picture of a global investment bank.

To help you determine your strengths and plan your career, summer analysts are matched with junior and senior mentors within your program's division, who provide advice and guidance throughout the summer. You'll also enjoy networking with the other Summer Analysts and full time employees at a variety of social events throughout the summer.

Equity Research - Summer Analyst

Deadline for application for the internship: December
Length of the program: 10 weeks

If you are a dynamic undergraduate looking for an intense and valuable introduction to the Equity Research arena, the Equity Research Summer Analyst Program may be for you. By working with one of our top-ranked Senior Research Analysts, you will gain an in-depth understanding of company analysis as well as the overall investment process. You will also have exposure to other divisions at CSFB, including CSFB's global sales force, equity traders and institutional clients.

After joining one of our outstanding research teams, you may work on projects involving financial analysis and investigative research. Equity Research summer analysts also have the opportunity to learn financial modeling and forecasting skills and to help produce research reports. In addition to your day-to-day responsibilities, you will be assigned an industry-specific project to work on throughout the summer. You will also be responsible for presenting on a stock as part of our summer stock pitch.

Training

The Equity Research Summer Training program begins with an intense one-week training period in New York where summer analysts participate in a capital markets overview, accounting review, and a research product overview. You will be trained on Bloomberg and learn CSFB technology systems and databases. You will tour the NYSE, and you'll meet with traders and salespeople from all of the various products.

Your learning experience will continue through the summer speaker series, where you will hear from senior management across the divisions. In addition, you will participate in networking events, community service and firm-wide events that will help ensure that you are exposed to all the areas within the bank.

To help you determine your strengths and plan your career, summer analysts are matched with a buddy and a mentor within Equity Research, who provide advice and guidance throughout the summer.

Summer Analyst – Asset Finance

Deadline for application for the internship: December
Length of the program: 10 weeks

Asset Finance Summer Analysts are investment bankers within the Fixed Income Division ("FID"). As a member of the Asset Finance Group, you will work within a team to help develop funding strategies for our clients. You'll also act as a liaison between our clients and the capital markets division, and execute transactions backed by a variety of asset classes, including: auto loans, credit card receivables, home equity loans, manufactured housing loans and student loans. Our clients cover many different industries and range from specialty finance firms to Fortune 500 companies.

During the 10-week program, summer analysts will have the opportunity to participate in all aspects of transaction execution: working with the client, performing due diligence, communicating with the FID trading floor, and managing the accountants, rating agencies and attorneys. They will also help perform any cash flow or financial analyses involved in completing the transaction. Finally, summer analysts will support the ongoing effort to build and strengthen client relationships by preparing marketing materials to pitch the ABS product to new clients as well as presenting new ideas to current clients. Summer analyst positions are located in New York.

Training and Content

The Fixed Income Dedicated Summer Program begins with an intense one-week training period in New York where summer analysts participate in a capital markets overview, a bond math review, and a library tour. You'll be trained on Bloomberg and learn CSFB technology systems and databases. You'll tour the NYSE, and you'll meet with traders and salespeople from all of the various products.

Your learning experience will continue through the summer speaker series, where you'll hear from senior employees across the divisions. In addition, you'll participate in networking events, a community service project, and firm-wide events that will help ensure that you are exposed to all the areas within the bank and understand the big picture of a global investment bank.

To help you determine your strengths and plan your career, summer analysts are matched with junior and senior mentors within Fixed Income, who provide advice and guidance throughout the summer.

Summer Analyst - Leveraged Finance Research

Deadline for application for the internship: December
Length of the program (in weeks): 10 weeks

Program Structure

Join our top-ranked Fixed Income Research department as a part of the Leveraged Finance Portfolio Strategy Team. Responsibilities will include:

Generating, analyzing and interpreting data related to the leveraged finance markets from a portfolio strategy, or macroscopic, perspective. Interface with buy-side clients, salespeople, traders and bankers to assist with the interpretation of market data related to the high yield, leveraged loan, structured product, (i.e. CDOs) and credit derivative markets.

Coordinating with a seven-person team to produce insightful analysis and research reports on topics such as event risk, defaults, performance, Western European high yield, leveraged loans and CDOs.

Conducting portfolio analytics for high yield mutual fund managers, assisting in industry and sector position recommendations and determining optimal asset allocations in forecasting market environments.

Training and Content

The Fixed Income Research program provides summer analysts with the foundation necessary for a successful summer experience. It begins with an intense one-week training period in New York where summer analysts participate in a capital markets overview, a bond math review, and a library tour. You'll be trained on Bloomberg and learn CSFB technology systems and databases. You'll tour the NYSE, and you'll meet with traders and salespeople from all of the various products.

After your first week of training, you'll hit the ground running, working to support a variety of desks within the Fixed Income Division. Your learning experience will continue through the summer speaker series, where you'll hear from senior employees across the divisions. In addition, you'll participate in networking events, community service, and firm-wide events that will help ensure that you are exposed to all the areas within the bank and understand the big picture of a global investment bank.

To help you determine your strengths and plan your career, summer analysts are matched with junior and senior mentors within Fixed Income, who provide advice and guidance throughout the summer. You'll also enjoy networking with the other Summer Analysts and full time employees at a variety of social events throughout the

Summer Analyst - Fixed Income Research

Deadline for application for the internship: December
Length of the program: 10 weeks

Program Structure

This summer you can join our top-ranked Fixed Income Research department as a Fixed Income Research Summer Analyst. By working with one of our widely respected Senior Research Analysts in Emerging Markets, Structured Products, Leveraged Finance, or Credit Research, you'll become knowledgeable about a research group and learn the fundamentals of research analysis. You will also gain exposure to other divisions of CSFB including our sales force, fixed income traders, investment bankers and institutional clients.

Training and Content

The Fixed Income Research program provides summer analysts with the foundation necessary for a successful summer experience. It begins with an intense one-week training period in New York where summer analysts participate in a capital markets overview, a bond math review, and a library tour. You'll be trained on Bloomberg and learn CSFB technology systems and databases. You'll tour the NYSE, and you'll meet with traders and salespeople from all of the various products.

After your first week of training, you'll hit the ground running, working to support a variety of desks within the Fixed Income Division. Your learning experience will continue through the summer speaker series, where you'll hear from senior employees across the divisions. In addition, you'll participate in networking events, community service, and firm-wide events that will help ensure that you are exposed to all the areas within the bank and understand the big picture of a global investment bank.

To help you determine your strengths and plan your career, summer analysts are matched with junior and senior mentors within Fixed Income, who provide advice and guidance throughout the summer. You'll also enjoy networking with the other Summer Analysts and full time employees at a variety of social events throughout the summer.

Summer Analyst – Real Estate Finance and Securitization

Deadline for application for the internship: December
Length of the program: 10 weeks

Program Structure

The Real Estate Finance & Securitization group's (REFS's) main product areas fall into the broad categories of real estate and real estate-related financial products – commercial mortgage-backed securities, for example. This group has a balance sheet of over $8 billion and operates in a principal capacity as well as providing investment banking services to corporate clients, institutions and publicly traded real estate companies.

REFS is organized into several operating teams:

Origination Group – Organized on a geographic basis in both the New York and Los Angeles offices, origination teams invest in debt and equity and combination financing for office, industrial, retail, hotel and multifamily, single tenant and other property types. Loans can be made for "whole loan" sale, securitization or balance sheet purposes.

Investment Banking – Provides advisory services for companies and institutions regarding their real estate activities. The work involves sale mandates, securitization, mergers and acquisitions, and other transactions.

Structured Finance – Focuses on securitization transactions and other "financially engineered" exits for REFS's investments.

Trading – Encompasses several units involving whole loans, commercial mortgage-backed securities (CMBS) and derivatives.

As a Summer Analyst, you will develop your understanding of the field by working on a variety of transactions. Summer Analyst positions are located in New York.

Training and Content

The Fixed Income Dedicated Summer Program begins with an intense one-week training period in New York where summer analysts participate in a capital markets overview, a bond math review, and a library tour. You'll be trained on Bloomberg and learn CSFB technology systems and databases. You'll tour the NYSE, and you'll meet with traders and salespeople from all of the various products.

Your learning experience will continue through the summer speaker series, where you'll hear from senior employees across the divisions. In addition, you'll participate in networking events, a community service project, and firm-wide events that will help ensure that you are exposed to all the areas within the bank and understand the big picture of a global investment bank.

To help you determine your strengths and plan your career, summer analysts are matched with junior and senior mentors within Fixed Income, who provide advice and guidance throughout the summer.

Scholarships

Douglas L. Paul Award for Achievement

Scholarship award amount: $5,000

CSFB will offer $5,000 scholarships to a number of college sophomores of African, Latino, and Native American descent. Recipients of the scholarships will be selected based on their academic excellence, leadership abilities, and interest in the financial services industry. In addition to monetary resources, students who receive the scholarship will have the opportunity to participate in our Wall Street Summer Immersion Program in New York. This unique 10-week placement provides students with an educational opportunity to learn about the various areas of an investment bank, with rotations in Equities, Fixed Income and Investment Banking.

CSFB/UNCF Scholarship

Scholarship award amount: $8,000

CSFB will offer two $8,000 scholarships, renewable for up to three years, to freshmen in college that attend a UNCF member school. In addition, students have the opportunity to intern with CSFB the summer between their sophomore and junior year.

Affinity Groups/Employee Networks

The Open Network in the Americas and Europe highlights an inclusive work culture in which lesbian, gay, bisexual and transgender (LGBT) employees can advance and succeed. Open Network members regularly assist in LGBT recruitment efforts and organize fundraising for local organizations serving the LGBT community. Speakers at Open Network events have included members of the U.S. Congress, actors and the world's leading experts on issues facing the LGBT community in the workplace.

CSFB America's Women's Network (AWN) helps create a supportive workplace where women can achieve their full potential. Activities include informal mentoring, networking events and presentations by internal and external women executives on topics including strategies for career planning and negotiating office politics. AWN also assist in recruitment efforts, sponsor fundraising events and host regular speaker series.

The Multicultural Resources Network (MRN) in the Americas and Europe is a forum where employees with various ethnic backgrounds and experiences can work together to develop professionally. MRN special events have included guest speakers, receptions, art exhibits, fundraisers and even cooking and dancing demonstrations showcasing the cultural heritage of our global community. MRN members are active in the firm's recruitment efforts and volunteer with a number of community organizations.

The Parents' Networks in the Americas and Europe provide information and support for current and expectant working parents, caregivers and their families. Along with guest speakers, the Networks host monthly "Bring Your Own Lunch" meetings to discuss topics of interest parents can use in child-rearing.

Entry-level Programs/Full-time Opportunities/Training Programs

Analyst - Corporate Investment Banking

Length of program: 2 years

Geographic locations of program: Full Time analyst opportunities may be available in our offices throughout North America including in New York, Chicago, Houston, Toronto, Los Angeles, Palo Alto and San Francisco.

As a first-year analyst, you will receive intensive classroom training for 7 weeks in New York, as part of a Investment Banking Training Program. Components of this training will include: an orientation to the firm, basics of accounting, corporate finance, financial modeling and valuation techniques, training on the firm's technology systems and the firm's database capabilities. You will learn key concepts integral to the career of an analyst and participate in a week long deal training seminar modeled after a real life scenario. The program also includes a variety of social events to facilitate networking among your peers and colleagues. In addition to our formal program, CSFB relies on on-the-job experience and continuous training to further develop an analyst's skills and knowledge.

Please describe any other educational components of this program: Students are provided with mentors.

Equities Research Associate

Length of program: Ongoing

Geographic locations of program: While most of our positions are in New York, we may have opportunities in our other offices in North America, including in San Francisco, Boston, Chicago and Houston.

As a first-year analyst you will receive intensive classroom training for 6 weeks in New York, as part of a Global Securities Training Program. Components of this training will include: an orientation to the firm, a financial math "boot camp," a buy-side class and capital markets overview, an accounting class, a valuation class, an overview of global debt and equity markets and instruments, an introduction to the sales, trading and research groups, and training in presentation skills and computer systems and applications. You'll also sit for the series 7 and 63 exams, and in certain instances the series 3 and 55. You will learn key concepts in sales and trading and participate in portfolio management simulations and trading games. At our many social and networking events, you'll make business contacts from around the globe. You will be paired with a buddy and mentor to make sure you have a smooth transition into the world of Equity Research.

Our stellar program is focused on continuous training and development, and we offer our Research Associates monthly skill-building workshops, best practices lunches, in-house CFA and GMAT training, accounting and writing workshops, and participation in the Mock Call Program. You must pass the Series 7 and 63 exams and are strongly encouraged to sit for all three levels of the CFA exam. Strong performers will be considered for promotion to Associate Analyst at the end of their third year.

Equities Sales & Trading

Length of program: Ongoing

Geographic location of program: New York

The Equity Analyst Program provides the foundation necessary for a successful career. Components of your training will include: an orientation to the firm, a financial math and accounting "boot camp," a buy-side class and capital markets overview, an accounting class, a valuation class, an overview of global debt and equity markets and instruments, an introduction to the sales, trading, research and structuring groups, and training in presentation skills and computer systems and applications.

You'll also sit for the series 7 and 63 exams, and in certain instances the series 3 and series 55. You will learn key concepts in sales and trading and participate in portfolio management trading games. At our many social and networking events, you'll make business contacts from around the globe. You'll also be paired with a mentor to make sure you have a smooth transition into the world of Equities.

Fixed Income Sales & Trading

Length of program: Ongoing
Geographic location of program: New York

As a first-year analyst, you will receive intensive classroom training for 11 weeks in New York, as part of a Global Securities Training Program. The Fixed Income Sales and Trading program provides analysts with the foundation necessary for a successful career. Components of your training will include: an orientation to the Firm, a financial math "boot camp," a buy-side class and capital markets overview, an accounting class, a valuation class, an overview of global debt and equity markets and instruments, an introduction to the sales, trading, research and structuring groups, and training in presentation skills and computer systems and applications.

You'll also sit for the series 7 and 63 exams, and in certain instances the series 3. You will learn key concepts in sales and trading and participate in portfolio management trading games. At our many social and networking events, you'll make business contacts from around the globe. You'll also be paired with a mentor to make sure you have a smooth transition into the world of Fixed Income.

Full-time Opportunities

Analyst: Asset finance

Asset Finance Analysts are investment bankers within the Fixed Income Division ("FID"). The financial structuring team focuses on developing and designing securitization structures for clients ranging from banks and insurance companies to consumer finance companies. The assets we focus on are consumer and commercial loans and leases, including automobile loans, credit card receivables, home equity loans, manufactured housing loans, student loans, equipment leases. Our team also structures and markets transactions indexed to esoteric risks including credit derivatives, regulatory assets and insurance payments

Training and Content

As a first-year analyst, you will receive intensive classroom training for 11 weeks in New York, as part of a Global Securities Training Program. Components of this training will include: an orientation to the Firm, a financial math "boot camp," a buy-side class and capital markets overview, an accounting class, a valuation class, an overview of global debt and equity markets and instruments, an introduction to the sales, trading, research and structuring groups, and training in presentation skills and computer systems and applications. You'll also sit for the series 7 and 63 exams, and in certain instances the series 3. You will learn key concepts in sales and trading and participate in portfolio management trading games. At our many social and networking events, you'll make business contacts from around the globe. You'll also be paired with a mentor to make sure you have a smooth transition into the world of Fixed Income.

Qualifications

Must be a degree candidate from a four-year college or university. Credit Suisse First Boston is noted for the diversity of its employees, but seeks candidates with a common set of abilities – highly motivated, a quantitative aptitude (statistics, math, econometrics or engineering background a plus) and computer/spread sheet literacy are essential. We are seeking candidates who possess strong problem solving abilities. While the focus of the financial structuring group is primarily analytical and quantitative, it is imperative that candidate have the ability to communicate technical concepts to a wide variety of individuals and can work effectively in a team environment. Strength in verbal and written communication, and computer literacy is essential to all that we do. We look for intelligent, driven and hardworking students with consistent leadership involvement in school activities and athletics, and proven interest in the financial sector arena.

Analyst: Fixed Income Leveraged Finance Research

Program Structure

Join our top-ranked Fixed Income Research department as a part of the Leveraged Finance Portfolio Strategy Team. Responsibilities will include:

> Generating, analyzing and interpreting data related to the leveraged finance markets from a portfolio strategy, or macroscopic, perspective. Interface with buy-side clients, salespeople, traders and bankers to assist with the interpretation

of market data related to the high yield, leveraged loan, structured product, (i.e. CDOs) and credit derivative markets.

Coordinating with a seven-person team to produce insightful analysis and research reports on topics such as event risk, defaults, performance, Western European high yield, leveraged loans and CDOs.

Conducting portfolio analytics for high yield mutual fund managers, assisting in industry and sector position recommendations and determining optimal asset allocations in forecasting market environments.

Training and Content

As a first-year analyst, you will receive intensive classroom training for 11 weeks in New York, as part of a Global Securities Training Program. Components of this training will include: an orientation to the firm, a financial math "boot camp," a buy-side class and capital markets overview, an accounting class, a valuation class, an overview of global debt and equity markets and instruments, an introduction to the sales, trading, research and structuring groups, and training in presentation skills and computer systems and applications. You'll also sit for the series 7 and 63 exams, and in certain instances the series 3. You will learn key concepts in sales and trading and participate in portfolio management trading games. At our many social and networking events, you'll make business contacts from around the globe. You'll also be paired with a mentor to make sure you have a smooth transition into the world of Fixed Income.

Qualifications

Must be a degree candidate from a four-year college or university. Credit Suisse First Boston is noted for the diversity of its employees, but seeks candidates with a common set of abilities – highly motivated, and creative individuals who have demonstrated academic achievement, specifically in finance, marketing, and accounting courses and have the ability to work independently and as a member of a team. Strength in verbal and written communication and computer literacy is essential to all that we do. We look for intelligent, driven and hardworking students with consistent leadership involvement in school activities and athletics, and proven interest in the financial sector arena. We look for a background in business, quantitative or economic related fields of work or study, strong quantitative, research, writing and communication skills, and a basic understanding of capital markets and statistics.

Analyst: Real Estate Finance & Securitization

The Real Estate Finance & Securitization (REFS) group's main product areas fall into the broad categories of real estate and real estate-related financial products – commercial mortgage-backed securities, for example. This group has a balance sheet of over $8 billion and operates in a principal capacity on an international basis, as well as providing investment banking services to corporate clients, institutions and publicly traded real estate companies.

REFS is organized into several operating teams:

Origination Group – Organized on a geographic basis in both the New York and Los Angeles offices, origination teams invest in debt and equity and combination financing for office, industrial, retail, hotel and multifamily, single tenant and other property types. Loans can be made for "whole loan" sale, securitization or balance sheet purposes.

Investment Banking – Provides advisory services for companies and institutions regarding their real estate activities. The work involves sale mandates, securitization, mergers and acquisitions, and other transactions.

Structured Finance – Focuses on securitization transactions and other "financially engineered" exits for REFS' investments.

Trading – Encompasses several units involving whole loans, commercial mortgage-backed securities (CMBS) and derivatives.

International – A new venture responsible for CSFB's real estate investments and loans in both Japan and non-Japan Asia, through two investment vehicles. A separate London-based group handles investments in Western Europe.

As a new analyst, you'll thoroughly develop your understanding of the field by first working as a generalist on a variety of transactions, and then developing your knowledge of specific products. After three years, high-performing analysts may be eligible for our "Fast Track" program, allowing them to be promoted directly to associate.

Training and Content

As a first-year analyst, you will receive intensive classroom training for 11 weeks in New York, as part of a Global Securities Training Program. Components of this training will include: an orientation to the Firm, a financial math "boot camp," a buy-side class and capital markets overview, an accounting class, a valuation class, an overview of global debt and equity markets and instruments, an introduction to the sales, trading, research and structuring groups, and training in presentation skills and computer systems and applications. You'll also sit for the series 7 and 63 exams, and in certain instances the series 3. You will learn key concepts in sales and trading and participate in portfolio management trading games. At our many social and networking events, you'll make business contacts from around the globe. You'll also be paired with a mentor to make sure you have a smooth transition into the world of Fixed Income.

Qualifications

Must be a degree candidate from a four-year college or university. Credit Suisse First Boston is noted for the diversity of its employees, but seeks candidates with a common set of abilities – highly motivated, and creative individuals who have demonstrated academic achievement, specifically in finance, marketing, and accounting courses and have the ability to work independently and as a member of a team. Strength in verbal and written communication, and computer literacy is essential to all that we do. We look for intelligent, driven and hardworking students with consistent leadership involvement in school activities and athletics, and proven interest in the financial sector arena.

Analyst: Asset Finance Structuring

Technical analyst for the Asset Finance Group will be responsible for collateral analysis in the origination of asset-backed securities and in M&A activity related to consumer finance and loan portfolios. The Asset Finance Group focuses on the securitization of consumer and commercial loans and leases, including automobile loans, credit card receivables, home equity loans, manufactured housing loans, student loans, equipment leases and similar assets. It also structures and markets transactions indexed to esoteric risks including credit derivatives, regulatory assets and insurance payments.

As a Technical analyst, you will interact closely with small deal teams and apply your technical skills in an intense and demanding environment. Responsibilities include working with issuers, rating agencies and accounting firms. The final product appears in marketing material delivered to investors. You will have significant interaction with other members of a deal team and our clients. You can expect to work on 20 to 25 transactions per year. The position provides an opportunity to develop your skills in a challenging environment.

Training and Content

As a first-year analyst, you will receive intensive classroom training for 11 weeks in New York, as part of a Global Securities Training Program. Components of this training will include: an orientation to the firm, a financial math "boot camp," a buy-side class and capital markets overview, an accounting class, a valuation class, an overview of global debt and equity markets and instruments, an introduction to the sales, trading, research and structuring groups, and training in presentation skills and computer systems and applications. You'll also sit for the series 7 and 63 exams, and in certain instances the series 3. You will learn key concepts in sales and trading and participate in portfolio management trading games. At our many social and networking events, you'll make business contacts from around the globe. You'll also be paired with a mentor to make sure you have a smooth transition into the world of Fixed Income.

Qualifications

Must be a degree candidate from a four-year college or university. Credit Suisse First Boston is noted for the diversity of its employees, but seeks candidates with a common set of abilities – highly motivated, a quantitative aptitude (statistics, math, econometrics or engineering background a plus) and computer/spread sheet literacy are essential. We are seeking candidates who possess strong problem solving abilities. While the focus of the financial structuring group is primarily analytical and quantitative, it is imperative that candidate have the ability to communicate technical concepts to a wide variety of individuals and can work effectively in a team environment. Strength in verbal and written communication, and computer literacy is essential to all that we do. We look for intelligent, driven and hardworking students with consistent leadership involvement in school activities and athletics, and proven interest in the financial sector arena.

Application

All interested candidates MUST send their resume and cover letter to securities.recruiting@csfb.com by March 1st for consideration.

Analyst: Fixed Income Research

Program Structure

Join our top-ranked Fixed Income Research department as a Fixed Income Research Analyst. By working with one of our widely respected Senior Research Analysts in

Emerging Markets, Structured Products, Leveraged Finance, or Credit Research, you'll become knowledgeable about a research group and learn the fundamentals of research analysis. You will also gain exposure to other divisions of CSFB including: our sales force, fixed income traders, investment bankers and institutional clients.

Training and Content

As a first-year Analyst, you will receive intensive classroom training for 11 weeks in New York, as part of a Global Securities Training Program. Components of this training will include: an orientation to the Firm, a financial math "boot camp," a buy-side class and capital markets overview, an accounting class, a valuation class, an overview of global debt and equity markets and instruments, an introduction to the sales, trading, research and structuring groups, and training in presentation skills and computer systems and applications. You'll also sit for the series 7 and 63 exams, and in certain instances the series 3. You will learn key concepts in sales and trading and participate in portfolio management trading games. At our many social and networking events, you'll make business contacts from around the globe. You'll also be paired with a mentor to make sure you have a smooth transition into the world of Fixed Income.

Qualifications

Must be a degree candidate from a four-year college or university. Credit Suisse First Boston is noted for the diversity of its employees, but seeks candidates with a common set of abilities – highly motivated, and creative individuals who have demonstrated academic achievement, specifically in finance, marketing and accounting courses and have the ability to work independently and as a member of a team. Strength in verbal and written communication, and computer literacy is essential to all that we do. We look for intelligent, driven and hardworking students with consistent leadership involvement in school activities and athletics, and proven interest in the financial sector arena. We look for a background in business, quantitative or economic related fields of work or study, strong quantitative, research, writing and communication skills, and a basic understanding of capital markets and statistics. Some language skills are required for certain research groups.

Diversity Mission Statement

CSFB's Global Inclusion and Diversity mission is to create an inclusive culture whereby:

- Employees' differences are valued and leveraged for the benefit of the business
- Employees are able to realize their full potential
- Employees are treated with dignity and respect

Additional Information

CSFB is dedicated to attracting, developing and retaining the best people in our industry. We bring together individuals of different genders, races, ages, nationalities, religions, sexual orientations and disabilities to create a world-class team of financial service professionals.

At the core of CSFB's philosophy of inclusion is the firm's Global Dignity at Work Policy – a set of conduct guidelines that apply to all employees worldwide. This policy ensures that diversity, inclusiveness and dignity in the workplace are everyone's responsibility. These enduring values are part of the very fabric of our business. They shape the way we hire, develop, and promote employees, and they guide us in the way we treat one another.

Your vision: **To reach for the top.**
Our promise: **Lifting you even higher.**

You thrive on success and you know just how far your talent will take you. We do too. That's why at Deutsche Bank, you'll be given the opportunity to realize your greatest ambitions. As one of the world's leading financial institutions, we have the platform to take your career higher. You will be part of an innovative, modern culture that celebrates achievement.

Expect the better career. Find out more at www.db.com/careers

A Passion to Perform. **Deutsche Bank** /

Deutsche Bank

60 Wall Street
New York, NY 10005
Phone: (212) 250-2500
www.db.com

The Stats

Revenue (FYE 12/04): 21.9 billion Euro
Net Income: 2.5 billion Euro
No. of Employees: 65,400

Diversity at Deutsche Bank

Deutsche Bank has been at the forefront of investment and retail banking in Europe for over 130 years. Its global footprint has now extended to cover over 76 countries and 13 million clients, providing a range of financial services to corporations, governments, agencies and private individuals and institutions. Some may be surprised to learn that the bank has been established in the Americas since the nineteenth century and began independent operations in the U.S. in 1978. In 1999 Deutsche Bank acquired Bankers Trust, broadening its product range and increasing its immersion in the U.S. marketplace. As a further show of commitment to the U.S. market, in October 2001 Deutsche Bank obtained a U.S. listing for its shares on the New York Stock Exchange and now employs 20% of its staff in the Americas.

At Deutsche Bank, we are committed to recruiting, retaining and developing diverse talent. We think of diversity in its broadest sense, embracing all of those differences that make up the exciting, challenging world in which we live. These include age, culture, ethnicity, gender, nationality, personality type, physical ability, religion, sexual orientation and work style.

A homogeneous workforce does not generate new ways of thinking. Diverse perspectives foster innovation and creativity. They enable us to build teams with a unique range of capabilities that can win the trust of our most demanding clients. They enhance our ability to respond to global business issues and provide innovative, superior solutions. That's why, for us, diversity is a business imperative, improving performance for clients, employees and shareholders alike.

Recognizing diversity is important, but not enough on its own. That is why we have invested in diversity, embedding it into the fabric of our organization. Deutsche Bank leverages its diversity and fosters a work environment that attracts, develops and retains a diverse pool of talent.

Our global graduate recruitment strategy aims to provide the Bank with a diverse graduate pipeline. We partner with a number of organizations and student clubs on the graduate and undergraduate levels to source diverse talent. Through our internship programs, we offer talented minority and female students at the high school and undergraduate levels the opportunity to experience the world of investment banking by partnering with several minority organizations in various regions. Many of our sponsorships and activities are educational and aimed to increase industry awareness, enabling us to perform outreach to a truly diverse audience who may not have previously considered a career in banking.

We provide opportunities for an open exchange of experiences and ideas across all levels of the Bank through our employee networks. For further information on our diversity initiatives and our firm, please visit our website at: www.db.com\careers.

LOOK BEYOND THE OBVIOUS.

You're an ideas person. You're open to new approaches. And you look beyond the obvious. At Goldman Sachs, we value people just like you. People who are ready to express their personality, share their ideas, and put their creativity to work. So if you're looking for a place where individuality is welcomed, look no further.

Goldman Sachs is an equal opportunity employer.

GS.COM/CAREERS

Goldman Sachs

Goldman, Sachs & Co.

85 Broad Street
New York, NY 10004
www.gs.com

Locations

Atlanta • Boston • Chicago • Dallas • George Town • Houston • Jersey City • Los Angeles • Melbourne • Mexico City • Miami • New York • Philadelphia • Princeton • Salt Lake City • San Francisco • Seattle • Tampa • Washington D.C.

Auckland • Bangalore • Bangkok • Beijing • Buenos Aires • Calgary • Dublin • Frankfurt • Geneva • Hong Kong • Johannes • Madrid • Milan • Moscow • Paris • Seoul • Shanghai • Singapore • Stockholm • Sao Paulo • Sydney • Taipei • Tokyo • Toronto • Zurich

The Stats

Revenue (2004): $20.55 billion (worldwide)

Contact Information

Contact Person: Martin Rodriguez, Associate

Diversity Team Leader: Melinda Wolfe, Managing Director, Global Head of Global Leadership and Diversity

Diversity Campus Recruiting Team Leader: Lance LaVergne, Vice President, Head of Americas Firmwide Diversity Recruiting

Diversity URLs:
www.gs.com/our_firm/our_culture/global_leadership_and_diversity/index.html

www.gs.com/careers/about_goldman_sachs/diversity/

Strategic Plan and Diversity Leadership

How does the firm's leadership communicate the importance of diversity to everyone at the firm?
E-mails, web site, meetings, workshops, newsletters and town halls

Who has primary responsibility for leading overall diversity initiatives at your firm?
Melinda Wolfe, Managing Director, Global Head of Global Leadership and Diversity

Who has primary responsibility for diversity recruiting initiatives at your firm, if different from?
Lance LaVergne, Vice President, (Head of Americas Firmwide Diversity Recruiting)

Does your firm currently have a diversity committee? Yes

If yes, does the committee's representation include one or more members of the firm's management/executive committee (or the equivalent)? Yes

If yes, how many senior managers are on the committee, and how often did the committee convene in furtherance of the firm's diversity initiatives in 2004?)

Total senior managers on committee: 21
Number of diversity meetings annually: Quarterly

If you have more than one diversity committee, please list.
Firmwide Diversity Committee, European Diversity Committee

Does the committee(s) and/or diversity leader establish and set goals or objectives consistent with management's priorities? Yes

Has the firm undertaken a formal or informal diversity program or set of initiatives aimed at increasing the diversity of the firm? Yes, formal

How often does the firm's management review the firm's diversity progress/results? Quarterly

How is the firm's diversity committee(s) and/or firm management held accountable for achieving results?
Senior management reports to the Board of Directors annually on the state of the firm's diversity initiatives.

Are the members of the diversity committee or committees involved in diversity activities?

Members of the diversity committees serve as senior sponsors for the employee networks. They serve as board members and active volunteers with organizations that serve underrepresented groups, such as the Jackie Robinson Foundation, Prep for Prep, Posse Foundation, and LEAD. They also actively mentor professionals from underrepresented groups and are involved in our recruiting efforts at HBCUs. Several of them also hold the title of Summer Diversity Champions and lead or sponsor training sessions such as Goldman Sachs Person by Person (GSPP) Diversity Training.

Recruitment of New Analysts and Associates

On-campus

Please list the schools at which your firm recruits.

- *Ivy League schools:* Harvard University, Princeton University, University of Pennsylvania, Columbia University, Brown University, Dartmouth College, Yale University, Cornell University

- *Public state schools:* University of Illinois, University of Indiana, University of California-Los Angeles, University of California-Berkeley, University of Michigan, University of Virginia, University of Texas, Rutgers University, City University of New York-Baruch College

- *Private schools:* Stanford, New York University, University of Chicago, Northwestern, Duke University, Georgetown University, Massachusetts Institute of Technology, Boston College, Williams College, Villanova University, St. John's University, Pace University, University of Notre Dame, Middlebury College, Carnegie Mellon University, Florida International University, University of Southern California, Florida International University

- *Historically Black colleges and universities (HBCUs):* Howard University, Morehouse College, Spelman College, Florida A&M University

- *Women's colleges:* Barnard College, Wellesley College, Smith College, Mt. Holyoke College

Of the schools that you listed above, do you have any special outreach efforts directed to encourage minority students to consider your firm?

- Host receptions for minority students
- Conferences
- Host and sponsor various student club conferences across campus recruiting schools
- Advertise in minority student association publications
- Participate in/host minority student job fairs
- Sponsor minority student association events
- Firm's professionals participate on career panels at school
- Outreach to leadership of minority student organizations
- Scholarships or intern/fellowships for minority students
- Sponsors and supporters of Robert Toigo Foundation, Consortium for Graduate Study in Management, Forte Foundation, Management Leadership for Tomorrow, National Hispanic Business Association
- Host workshops for graduate and undergradutate students through programs such as undergraduate and MBA camps.

Professional Recruiting

What activities does the firm undertake to attract women and minorities?

- Partner programs with women and minority banking associations
- Conferences: National Black MBA (NBMBAA), National Society of Hispanic MBAs (NSHMBA), National Society of Black Engineers (NSBE), Society of Hispanic Engineers (SHPE), National Association of Black Accountants (NABA), Association of Latin Professionals in Finance and Accounting (ALPFA), Hispanic Alliance for Career Enhancement (HACE), Consortium for Graduate Study in Management (CGSM), Society of Women Engineers (SWE)
- Participate at minority job fairs
- Seek referrals from other professionals

Do you use executive recruiting/search firms to seek to identify new diversity hires? Yes

Internships

Summer Analyst Program

Deadline for application for the internship: Winter 2005, varies from school to school
Number of interns in the program in summer 2004: 915 (worldwide)
Length of the program (in weeks): 10 weeks
Program web site: www.gs.com/careers

Please describe the internship program, including departments hiring, intern responsibilities, qualifications for the program and any other details you feel are relevant.

Summer Analysts join a 10 week comprehensive program, where they are given the opportunity to learn critical business skills, while gaining fundamental experience in their respective divisions. Goldman Sachs seeks highly motivated candidates who have demonstrated outstanding achievements in academic and extracurricular activities. We are looking for self-motivated, team players who have excellent organizational and communication skills. While a background in finance or accounting is not required, candidates should have an interest in business and financial markets.

The following divisions hire summer analysts: Equities, Fixed Income, Currency & Commodities, Financing Group, Finance (includes Controllers, Credit & Corporate Treasury and Firmwide Risk), Global Investment Research, Human Capital Management, Investment Banking/Corporate Finance, Investment Management-Asset Management, Investment Management-Private Wealth Management, Global Compliance, Legal & Management Controls, Merchant Banking/Private Equity, Operations (includes Corporate Services and Global Operations) and Technology. Please visit our web site for specific divisional overviews at: www.gs.com.

Scholarships

Scholarship for Excellence

Deadline for application for the scholarship program: December, 2005
Scholarship award amount: $5,000 – sophomores, with an opportunity to be considered for an additional $7,500 in their junior year; $7,500 – juniors
Program web site or other contact information for scholarship:
cindy.joseph@gs.com
Contact: Cindy Joseph
Phone: 917-343-8562

Web site: www.gs.com/careers/about_goldman_sachs/diversity/internships_scholarships/index.html

Please describe the scholarship program, including basic requirements, eligibility, length of program and any other details you feel are relevant.

The Goldman Sachs Scholarship for Excellence Program was established in 1994 and is an integral part of our diversity recruiting effort, helping to attract undergraduate students of Black, Hispanic and Native American heritage to careers at Goldman Sachs. Students of all majors and disciplines are encouraged to apply.

Recipients of the scholarship will receive:

- **Sophomores** – $5,000 scholarship to cover tuition and fees with an opportunity to receive an additional award upon successful completion of summer internship and offer to return for a second summer internship

- **Juniors** – $7,500 scholarship to cover tuition and fees

- An internship as a summer analyst, gaining insight into the financial services industry, the firm and our unique culture

- A coach/mentor that will help ensure a successful summer experience

- Exposure to senior level managers and participation in firmwide networking opportunities

Eligibility:

The following are criteria we consider when selecting our scholarship recipients:

- Enrollment at one of our recruiting schools as a current sophomore or junior
- Black, Hispanic or Native American heritage
- Minimum cumulative grade point average of 3.4 or above on a 4.0 scale
- Interest in the financial services industry
- Community involvement – service to campus and community
- Demonstrated leadership and teamwork capabilities

Affinity Groups/Employee Networks

Firmwide Black Network

Name of affinity group leader: Tom Mattox, Gregg Gonsalves

The mission of the Goldman Sachs Firmwide Black Network is to enhance professional development and advancement opportunities for Black employees and to support recruitment and retention. The FBN also engages and advises senior business managers regarding the firm's diversity strategy and issues of importance to the firm's Black community.

The Goldman Sachs Firmwide Black Network ("FBN") was formally launched in October, 2001 to enrich the professional lives of Black employees and to assist the firm in identifying and addressing issues of importance to the firm's Black community. The FBN presents programs focusing on strategies and skills to catalyze professional advancement, and it sponsors events to promote awareness and understanding of the relationships between public policy and business challenges in the financial services industry. The FBN partners with senior leaders of the firm's businesses and diversity efforts to develop initiatives and sponsor activities that augment the firm's commitment to strengthen the franchise through its people. With a diverse workforce becoming increasingly more important in the firm's ability to continue to compete effectively in a global environment, the FBN represents a critical resource in supporting the firm's business principles and objectives.

Firmwide Hispanic/Latin Network (FHLN)

Name of affinity group leader: Marina Roesler

The mission of the Goldman Sachs Firmwide Hispanic/Latin Network will be to focus on recruitment, retention, promotion, development and advocacy for the Goldman Sachs Hispanic/Latin community.

This organization is dedicated to inspiring the Hispanic/Latin community to actively participate in leadership development and community service. It will foster an inclusive business climate that leverages the unique talents, perspectives and experiences of the group. The network will create a sense of community and cultural awareness among the Hispanics/Latinos and the broader population of the firm. We will create a work environment that enables people to do their best work by establishing informal networks, mentoring, mobility and communication.

Asian Professionals Network (APN)

Name of affinity group leader: Jacqueline Liau

The mission of the Asian Professionals Network ("APN") is to act as a bridge in the firm for the recruitment, retention, development and promotion of Asian professionals.

The organization serves as a channel to shares ideas, raise awareness and create a sense of collaboration and community among Asian professionals. It provides a forum to promote the diverse achievements and contributions of Asian professionals to the firm. The network also works to enhance the Goldman experience for Asian professionals by implementing programs that will foster greater interaction with the broader community. The APN aims to energize, amplify and empower Asian professionals to make greater contributions to the firm and to the outside community.

Gay and Lesbian Network

Name of affinity group leaders: Robert Barry, Arden Hoffman

As part of Goldman Sachs' commitment to diversity, the Gay and Lesbian Network's mission is to advocate a work environment that respects, welcomes and supports lesbian, gay, bisexual and transgender professionals, and empowers them to perform to their fullest potential and contribute to the greater goals of the firm.

The organization works to increase the visibility of openly lesbian, gay, bisexual and transgender (LGBT) employees at Goldman Sachs, and to foster greater inclusion within the greater Goldman Sachs community. It provides a global, supportive, professional network that promotes mentoring and a sense of community. It also advocates on diversity issues related to sexual orientation and gender identity within the firm, and serves as an information resource to management on LGBT issues.

Firmwide Women's Network

Name of affinity group leader: Luciana Miranda

The Firmwide Women's Network mission is to recruit, retain and develop women professionals at Goldman Sachs, and to increase their representation at senior levels.

Entry-level Programs/Full-time Opportunities/Training Programs

Full-time Analyst Program

Length of program: Average of 2-3 years

Geographic location(s) of program: Opportunities are available at several of our global offices.

Most analysts join two-to-three year formal training programs. The main purpose of these programs is to help our analysts learn critical business skills while gaining fundamental skills in their respective divisions. Goldman Sachs seeks highly motivated candidates who have demonstrated outstanding achievements in academic and extracurricular activities. We are looking for self-motivated, team players who have excellent organizational and communication skills. While a background in finance or accounting is not required, candidates should have an interest in business and financial markets.

Goldman Sachs hires full-time analysts for the following divisions: Equities, Fixed Income, Currency & Commodities, Financing Group, Finance (includes Controllers, Credit & Corporate Treasury and Firmwide Risk), Global Investment Research, Human Capital Management, Investment Banking/Corporate Finance, Investment Management-Asset Management, Investment Management – Private Wealth Management, Global Compliance, Legal & Management Controls, Merchant Banking/Private Equity, Operations (includes Corporate Services and Global

Operations), and Technology. Please visit our web site for specific divisional overviews at: www.gs.com.

Diversity Mission Statement

Goldman Sachs aims to be the employer, advisor, and investment of choice by attracting and retaining the best and most diverse talent. Through our leadership and diversity efforts, including the affinity network program, we work to provide a supportive and inclusive environment where all individuals, regardless of gender, race, ethnicity, national origin, sexual orientation, gender identity, disability or other classification can maximize their full potential, which in turn leads to strengthening the firm's position as a leader in the industry.

To manage diversity well, we have to manage people well. We realize that successful formal processes have a particularly positive influence on women, historically underrepresented groups and non-U.S. nationals. The Office of Global Leadership and Diversity reinforces our culture of meritocracy by advancing leadership and management skills, and integrating diversity considerations into our key business and people processes, such as recruiting, training, career development and other retention strategies.

We leverage FOUR CATALYSTS to affect change:

- **Leadership Commitment**
- **Education & Training**
- **Communication & Involvement**
- **Measurement & Accountability**

Additional Information

At Goldman Sachs we recognize that having a diverse workforce encourages increased creativity and innovation. This is crucial to improved performance and continued business success. To that end, we are committed to creating an environment that values diversity and promotes inclusion. Goldman Sachs recruits individuals from diverse cultures and backgrounds. The result is a wealth of talent and creativity where exceptional individuals work together to provide a world-class service to a broad spectrum of corporate, government, institutional and private clients.

In our search for outstanding individuals we partner with organizations promoting diversity. Through our work with INROADS, Sponsors for Educational Opportunity, the Jackie Robinson Foundation, the Forte Foundation, the Employers Forum on Disability and others, we increase our commitment to recruiting women, students from ethnic minorities and those with disabilities.

Further, we have initiated and manage a number of programs designed to increase awareness of the firm and our industry. These programs allow us to offer academic scholarships, educational opportunities, summer internships and full-time positions to many outstanding students. Not of all of these students have a finance or business background; we actively seek candidates from a broad array of academic disciplines and concentrations such as liberal arts, applied math, sciences and engineering, in order to reach a wide spectrum of strong candidates.

We invite you to take a closer look at our firm and learn more about the different programs and opportunities available to you at www.gs.com/careers.

Harris

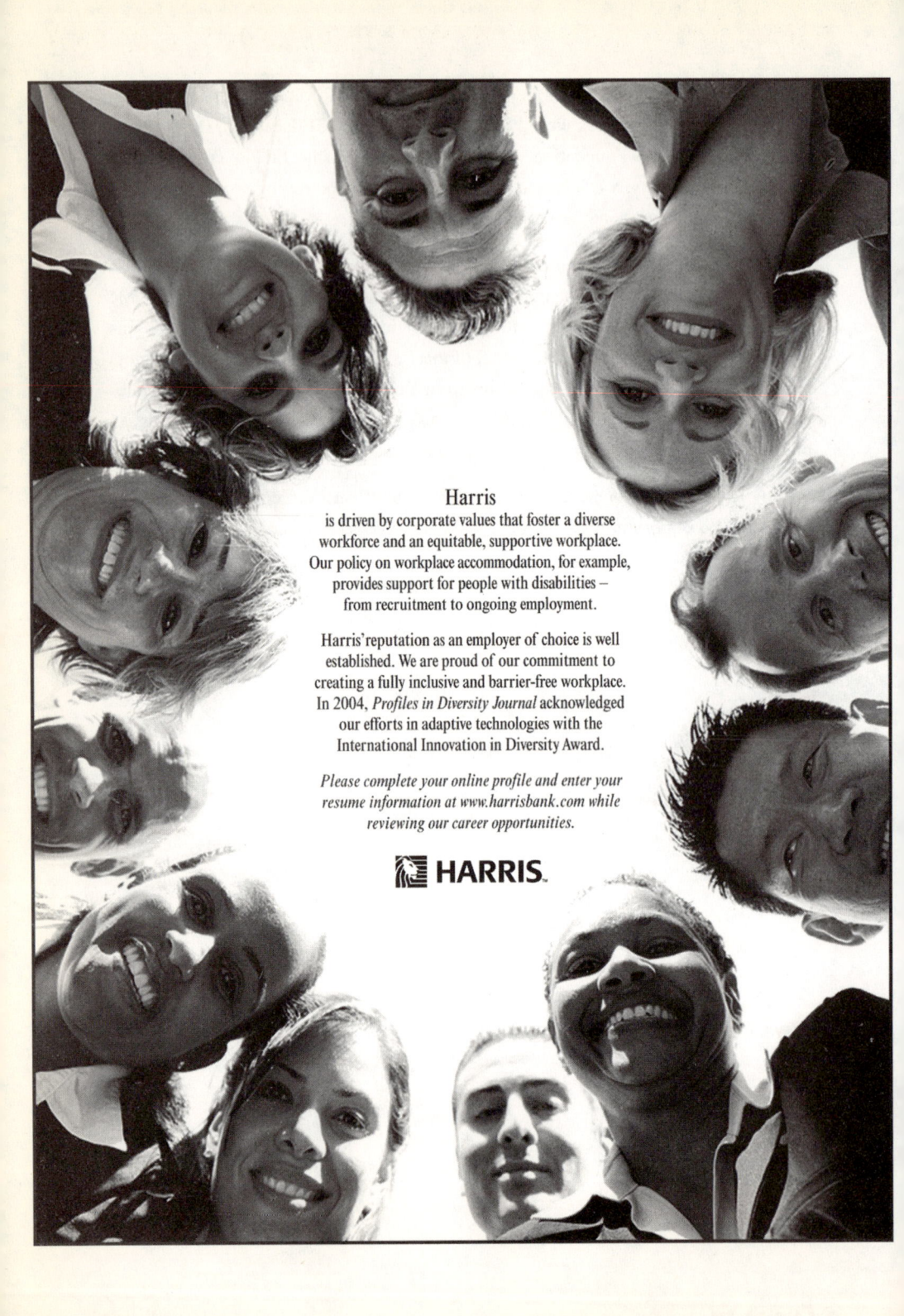

is driven by corporate values that foster a diverse workforce and an equitable, supportive workplace. Our policy on workplace accommodation, for example, provides support for people with disabilities – from recruitment to ongoing employment.

Harris' reputation as an employer of choice is well established. We are proud of our commitment to creating a fully inclusive and barrier-free workplace. In 2004, *Profiles in Diversity Journal* acknowledged our efforts in adaptive technologies with the International Innovation in Diversity Award.

Please complete your online profile and enter your resume information at www.harrisbank.com while reviewing our career opportunities.

HARRIS

Harris (a part of BMO Financial Group)

111 West Monroe Street
Chicago, IL 60603
Phone: 312-461-2000
www.harrisbank.com

Locations

BMO Financial Group (including Harris) has over 34,000 employees with branches located worldwide, in countries such as Canada, United States, England, Barbados, Bermuda, Ireland, Hong Kong and Mexico.

The Stats

Revenue (2004): $58.8 billion (U.S.)
Revenue (2004): $265 billion (worldwide)

Contact Information

Diversity Contact:
Robye Smith, Vice-President, Senior Manager, Governance and Diversity Business, Partner for Investment Banking Group and Private Client Group – U.S.

Diversity Team Leader:
Marjorie Paddock, Co-Director, Diversity & Workplace Equity

Diversity Campus Recruiting Team Leader: Hewitt Recruiting Solutions

Business Information

Applicable areas within Harris include:

Harris Nesbitt offers clients complete financial solutions across the entire balance sheet, including treasury services, foreign exchange, trade finance, cash management, corporate lending, securitization and public and private debt and equity underwriting. The group also offers leading financial advisory services in mergers and acquisitions and restructurings, while providing our investing clients with industry-leading research, sales and trading services.

Within Harris Private Banking and Investing Services:

Harrisdirect
Harrisdirect provides self-directed investors with an award-winning[1] trading platform and a broad range of investment options, including stocks, options, bonds, CDs and mutual funds.

Harrisdirect Advisory Services
Harrisdirect Advisory Services provides you with the ongoing guidance of experienced investment professionals. As a Harrisdirect client, you will receive objective and customized investment advice based on your specific needs.

Harris Private Bank
Harris Private Bank helps high net worth clients realize financial and lifestyle goals with custom-tailored solutions delivered with the highest level of service.

Harris myCFO Inc.
Harris myCFO serves clients of significant wealth and complex needs who are looking for a financial solution that combines the finest personal service, best-in-class solutions and advanced technology.

Sullivan, Bruyette, Speros & Blayney Inc. (SBSB)
SBSB provides full-service financial planning, portfolio management and tax services to high net worth clients.

Harris Insight® Funds
The skilled investment teams behind the Harris Insight Funds believe that consistent investment performance requires discipline, focus, knowledge and the finest informational resources available.

HIM Monegy Inc.
HIM Monegy is a subsidiary of Chicago-based Harris Investment Management, Inc. and operates within BMO Financial Group. HIM Monegy consists of an experienced group of professionals dedicated to managing credit risk assets (corporate bonds, loans and synthetic securities) for third party institutional investors.

Strategic Plan and Diversity Leadership

How does the firm's leadership communicate the importance of diversity to everyone at the firm?
At Harris, employee communication is a critical platform within a wider employee engagement strategy. One way of maintaining high levels of engagement is through open channels of communication.

Top Down Communication: Harris' President and CEO, Frank Techar, provides monthly updates and context on what is taking place throughout the organization. His messages not only inform, but also help employees take proactive measures to enhance customer experiences, improve productivity and increase company performance. The organization's senior-most executives also participated in a transnational tour to detail the year's strategic objectives. Senior executives across the organization also participate in "fireside chats" with groups of employees across the bank.

Bottom Up Communication: Frequently, employees participate in the Lunch and Learn program initiated and organized by employee affinity groups and featuring senior executives on topics such as career paths and the importance of finding and being mentors.

Communication Vehicles: One of the most proven and effective methods for communicating messages to employees is through the intranet, which is updated with relevant company news every day. Harris also utilizes company newsletters, which feature current articles and updates to policies and programs. The newsletter (@work) is delivered on a monthly basis and is posted internally on Harris websites. @work features news on upcoming corporate programs as well as features on involvement in the community, retirements and updates on the organization's progress against objectives set by the Annual Employee Survey. A local weekly newsletter, Spectrum P.S., keeps employees abreast of company news, events, employee milestones and educational programs taking place within the organization.

Feedback Mechanisms: Recognizing that communication is a two-way street, senior executives encourage employees to provide feedback in several ways. Since his arrival at Harris, Frank Techar has embarked on an employee tour, visiting many Harris locations and meeting staff at each stop. In informal settings, Techar meets with employees at all levels and discusses strategies and initiatives for the upcoming year. His tours provide a forum for employees to discuss what has actually been happening in their specific areas and what is at the forefront of their minds.

Who has primary responsibility for leading overall diversity initiatives at your firm?
Frank Techar, President and CEO Harris and Chair of the CEO's Council on the Equitable Workforce.

Who has primary responsibility for diversity recruiting initiatives at your firm, if different from the above?
Hewitt Recruiting Solutions

Does your firm currently have a diversity committee? Yes

If yes, does the committee's representation include one or more members of the firm's management/executive committee (or the equivalent)? Yes

If yes, how many senior managers are on the committee, and how often did the committee convene in furtherance of the firm's diversity initiatives in 2004?

Total senior managers on committee: at least one per committee
Number of diversity meetings annually: Each diversity council meets quarterly at a minimum with many meetings monthly.

If you have more than one diversity committee, please list.
Articulating Harris' corporate values to every employee within the organization is responsibility of the CEO's Council on an Equitable Workplace (whose members include Chair Frank Techar, President and CEO of Harris, Tony Comper, the President and CEO of BMO Financial Group, the Vice-Chairs of each of the lines of business, the Senior Executive Vice-President of Human Resources, the Head of the Office of Strategic Management and BMO's Chief Financial Officer). This group meets quarterly to review progress and to advise on what needs to be done to ensure the organization reaches its workplace equity goals. They are supported by Diversity Advisory Councils (19 in the U.S. and 8 in Canada) and Affinity Groups (4 in the U.S. and 6 in Canada), which draw members from all levels of the organization. These groups fulfill a grassroots role by collecting and disseminating information to provide advice and counsel to business leaders.

Diversity Councils include employees who are actively involved in increasing awareness and advocating for diversity and workplace equity. Each Council has an executive sponsor who is responsible for providing leadership for diversity and workplace equity at the local and divisional levels. Council members serve as employees' direct link to our diversity and workplace equity initiatives. Both the Investment Banking Group and Private Client Group have very active Diversity Councils.

The Diversity Councils have two fundamental roles: to bring the voice of the employee into goal-setting discussions and to act as grassroots champions of change. They function as ambassadors for diversity and workplace equity-providing advice and support to the business unit's executive team on issues related to the advancement of diversity and workplace equity and meeting regularly with employee groups to generate awareness around diversity and workplace equity initiatives.

Does the committee(s) and/or diversity leader establish and set goals or objectives consistent with management's priorities? Yes (see above).
Harris, a part of BMO Financial Group, is committed to creating a diverse workforce and an equitable, supportive and inclusive workplace.

Has the firm undertaken a formal or informal diversity program or set of initiatives aimed at increasing the diversity of the firm? Yes, formal

How often does the firm's management review the firm's diversity progress/results? Quarterly

How are the firm's diversity committee(s) and/or firm management held accountable for achieving results?
Through annual performance appraisals, executives are held accountable for meeting their diversity goals. The CEO's Council on the Equitable Workplace approved greater accountability for the achievement of executives' diversity and workplace equity qualitative and quantitative goals in the fall of 2000.

Additionally, diversity is included on Business Scorecards for Chicagoland Banking.

Are the members of the diversity committee or committees involved in diversity activities?
Harris' Diversity Council of Councils In addition to local Diversity Councils, an enterprise-wide Diversity Council, made up of one representative from each local Council and chaired by Harris Bank's CEO, provided a forum for sharing information and insight across the Councils while addressing enterprise-wide issues with a unified and consistent approach.

Harris Diversity Councils also participate in several Lunch and Learn sessions on a variety of topics such as Black History Month or Chinese New Year.

Recruitment of New Analysts and Associates

On-campus

Please list the schools at which you recruit.

- *Ivy League schools:* Princeton, Yale, Brown University
- *Public state schools:* University of Colorado
- *Private schools:* New York University, Rice University, University of Loyola University, DePaul University, Fordham University, Babson College
- *Historically Black Colleges and Universities (HBCUs):* No schools currently, but it is part of the organization's Diversity Strategic Plan
- *Hispanic Serving Institutions (HSIs):* No schools currently, but it is part of the organization's Diversity Strategic Plan
- *Native American Tribal Universities:* Arizona State University
- Other predominantly minority and/or women's colleges

Of the schools that you listed above, do you have any special outreach efforts directed to encourage minority students to consider your firm?

- Firm's professionals participate on career panels at school
- Outreach to leadership of minority student organizations

Professional Recruiting

What activities does the firm undertake to attract women and minorities?

- Partner programs with women and minority banking associations
- Participate at minority job fairs
- Seek referrals from other professionals
- Utilize online job services

Participate in Diversity Job Fairs and career fairs for people with disabilities.

Utilize www.vault.com for job postings.

Do you use executive recruiting/search firms to seek to identify new diversity hires? Yes (Both)

> Carrington & Carrington (minority-owned executive recruiting firm)
> Salem Temporary Services (women-owned recruiting firm)

When larger executive search firms are used, Harris requests their diversity account manager.

Internships

Harris Summer Internship Program

> *Number of interns in the program in summer 2004:* Interns hired by the individual lines of business
>
> *Length of the program (in weeks):* Varies depending on the needs of the business and the college schedule of the summer hire
>
> *Web site for internship information:* Recruitment takes place through college placement offices

Scholarships

Harris' scholarship programs are under review at this time.

Affinity Groups/Employee Networks

Contact Robye Smith for Affinity Group related questions or visit www.harrisbank.com. U.S. Affinity Groups include:

Asian American Coalition of Employees

In 1998, a group of Asian American employees at Harris Bank formed AACE, the Asian American Coalition of Employees at Harris Bank. Their mission statement is to foster an environment that facilitates personal growth and professional advancement for Asian American employees in ways that complement the overall goals of BMO Financial Group. AACE does this by scheduling periodic events to provide an informal social setting for Asian American employees across the organization. They have also developed a successful mentoring program.

Hispanic Networking Group

Set up as an employee-based organization to support the career development and advancement of Latino employees, the Hispanic Networking Group (HNG) was established in 1994 as Latinos Profesionales en Acción. Recruitment, performance management, career development/training and recognition of Latino employees were among the top issues that surfaced during focus group sessions. The HNG's mission statement is to advocate and assist in the recognition, development and advancement of Latino employees in order to support BMO Financial Group in becoming a highly focused, highly selective client-centered organization. Recently, Canadian Latino employees have joined their colleagues in the U.S. making this a truly North American Affinity Group.

Lion's Pride GLBTS Affinity Group

Lion's Pride is an informal group of Gay, Lesbian, Bisexual, Transgender and Straight (GLBTS) employees. It seeks to be a forum for GLBTS employees to come together for support, mentoring, networking and career development within Harris Bank and BMO Financial Group. Lion's Pride ensures that GLBTS employees are treated equally and fairly in all matters and to bolster the success of all members in all business relationships with the GLBTS Community. It also acts as a liaison to Management and Employee Relations for information, issues and concerns of GLBTS employees.

African American League of Professionals

The African American League of Professionals stemmed from the Black Resource Team formed barely thirty years ago. When Harris created its mandate regarding the Diversity Advisory Councils, the Black Resource Team opened their Affinity Group to everyone and formed the African American League of Professionals. This group's mandate is to contribute to the success of Harris and BMO Financial Group by fostering an environment for African American employees where recognition, mentoring, career and personal development are consistently promoted through education, networking and community involvement.

Entry-level Programs/Full-time Opportunities/Training Programs

Relationship Manager Development Program

Length of program: 9 months
Geographic location(s) of program: Chicago

Please describe the training/training component of this program.
The program is designed to help Relationship Managers and play a vital role in their success by developing and maintaining strong ties with clients. Employees are exposed to a varied curriculum of classes, seminars, hands-on training and on-the-job experience. Employees will learn analysis skills required to perform credit analysis and provide financial advice.

Please describe any other educational components of this program.
Harris utilizes informal mentoring at all levels throughout the organization.

Diversity Mission Statement

We are committed to creating a diverse workforce, and an equitable, supportive workplace.

Additional Information

Developing an equitable and supportive workplace that reflects the diversity of the communities in which Harris does business is an objective that is explicitly aligned with strategic initiatives from the top and which is carefully measured and connected to performance.

Stemming from the information documented in the Task Forces [Advancement of Women (1991), Advancement of Aboriginal Employment (1992), Employment of People with Disabilities (1992) and the Advancement of Visible Minorities (1995)], the following programs and policies have ensured that Harris is an employer of choice. These elements define Harris as a best practice leader in diversity and workplace equity.

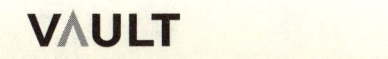

Corporate Values: These represent Harris' core beliefs. They stand as our collective commitment – to each other, to our customers, to our shareholders and the communities of which we are a part.

- We care about customers, shareholders, communities and each other.

- We draw our strength from the diversity of our people and our businesses.

- We insist upon respect for everyone and encourage all to have a voice.

- We keep our promises and stand accountable for our every action.

- We share information, learn and innovate to create consistently superior customer experiences.

Ethical Behaviour: First Principles: Annually, all Harris employees must re-read and sign a declaration attesting to their continuing compliance Harris' ethical guidelines, First Principles: Working with Integrity. This declaration sets out rules, procedures and expectations about ethical behavior. It asks: Is it fair? Is it right? Is it legal?

In-House Employee Assistance Program (EAP): Harris offers award-winning internal EAP services to employees, pensioners and their families. These services include personal counseling, childcare services, eldercare services, management consultation, trauma response, group support and solutions and information and resources.

Flexible Work Arrangements: Flexible work arrangements are employee-initiated, manager-approved arrangements that provide the opportunity for flexibility in determining when, where or how the work gets done.

- Flextime is the most straightforward option available. You simply shift the standard 7.5 hour work day to begin and end at times you and your manager find mutually acceptable.

- Flexible Work Week enables you to arrange, with your manager, a variation on the standard 7.5 hour day, 5-day work week. For example, you can compress the week into fewer but longer days. Or stretch it out over shorter days in a 6-day week.

- Permanent Part-time enables you to set up, with your manager, a regular schedule in which you work less than Harris' standard hours.

- Job Sharing enables you to arrange, with your manager, to share your job with one or more other permanent employees.

- Flexplace/Telecommuting enables you to arrange to work in another location, outside the office. For example, you could relocate to another Harris office, or set up a home office, where you would do some or almost all of your regular work.

Institute for Learning: The Institute for Learning (IFL), an offsite facility, is similar to a corporate university, and serves as the organization's strategic training and education base. The IFL includes state-of-the-art classroom facilities as well as hotel facilities and an employee lounge. There are satellite locations within the United States and employees are able to utilize the Toronto location as well.

Career Discovery Interactive Intranet Site: Harris has a leading edge web site, Career Discovery, which offers tools and resources to help us discover employee talents and engage in meaningful career conversations. Some features include Development Planning Guides, downloadable resume samples and links to career opportunities within Harris.

Annual Employee Survey: Harris uses the Annual Employee Survey (AES) to measure employee attitudes and opinions about workplace issues, including the enterprise's commitment to a diverse workforce and an equitable, supportive workplace. The AES plays a key role in ensuring that the employee voice is heard and taken seriously at all levels of the organization.

- Diversity Index (DI) – The DI is a compilation of questions that enables Harris to measure how well employees think we are doing in the area of diversity & workplace equity. These efforts enable managers to further assess and prioritize their diversity action plans and strategies.

JPMorgan Chase

270 Park Avenue
New York, NY 10017
Phone: 212-270-6000
Fax: 212-270-8380
www.jpmorganchase.com

Locations

New York, NY (HQ)
3,775 offices in over 50 countries

The Stats

Revenue (2004): $57.2 billion

Contact Information

Contact Person: Adriene K. Bruce, Diversity Recruiting Manager
E-mail: Adriene_k_bruce@jpmorgan.com
Campus Recruiting Team Leaders: Ellen Diverniero, Senior Vice President and Adriene K. Bruce, Vice President

Strategic Plan and Diversity Leadership

How does the firm's leadership communicate the importance of diversity to everyone at the firm?
E-mails to all employees worldwide; postings of news stories on company website; postings on diversity web site; diversity as an agenda item during employee town hall meetings; posters and lobby displays in most JPMC locations; interviews in monthly employee newsletter.

Who has primary responsibility for leading overall diversity initiatives at your firm?
Joy Bunson, Senior Vice President, Leadership & Organizational Development

Who has primary responsibility for diversity recruiting initiatives at your firm, if different from the above?
For entry-level recruiting, the person is Adriene K. Bruce, Vice President of University Relations

Does your firm currently have a diversity committee? Yes

If yes, does the committee's representation include one or more members of the firm's management/executive committee (or the equivalent)? Yes

If yes, how many senior managers are on the committee, and how often did the committee convene in furtherance of the firm's diversity initiatives in 2004?

Total senior managers on committee: 32
Diversity is on the agenda at every excecutive committee meeting.

If you have more than one diversity committee, please list.
We have one Corporate Diversity Council, chaired by JPMC Chairman & CEO Bill Harrison, with members of senior managers across the firm. In addition, each business and function has its own diversity council (estimated 50 additional councils).

Does the committee(s) and/or diversity leader establish and set goals or objectives consistent with management's priorities? Yes

Has the firm undertaken a formal or informal diversity program or set of initiatives aimed at increasing the diversity of the firm? Yes

How often does the firm's management review the firm's diversity progress/results? Monthly

How are the firm's diversity committee(s) and/or firm management held accountable for achieving results?
The Corporate Diversity Council manages using a diversity scorecard, metrics for which are reviewed at least monthly. These metrics are applied to an overall Corporate Scorecard, upon which senior managers' compensation is based. In addition, the firm's diversity metrics are discussed with the firm's Board of Directors.

Are the members of the diversity committee or committees involved in diversity activities? Yes

If so, list and describe some of those activities.

- Membership on business diversity councils.
- Sponsorship of business or site-specific diversity events, many in recognition of diversity recognition months (such as Women's History Month or Asia-Pacific American Month)
- Mentoring
- Leadership roles with Employee Networking Groups
- Participating in college recruiting
- Sponsorship of "fireside chats" with key employee groups

Recruitment of New Analysts and Associates

On-campus

Please list the schools at which your school recruits.

- *Ivy League schools:* All schools in the Ivy League
- *Public state schools:* Too numerous to list – more than 20
- *Private schools:* Too numerous to list – more than 30
- *Historically Black Colleges and Universities (HBCUs):* Florida A&M, Howard, Morehouse, Spelman, and several others

Hispanic Serving Institutions (HSIs): UT El Paso, UT San Antonio, UT Pan American, Texas A&M, UCLA, University of Miami, City College of NY
- *Predominantly minority and/or women's colleges:* Numerous women's colleges and UNCF institutions.

Of the schools that you listed above, do you have any special outreach efforts directed to encourage minority students to consider your firm.

- Hold a reception for minority students

- Conferences: We participate in a variety of conferences and initiatives hosted by schools and other organizations. For instance, we participate in MBA Jump Start, the Forte Foundation's annual conference, the annual conference held by the Office of Career Opportunities for Students with Disabilities, The Consortium Annual Conference, the annual INROADS Best Practices Conference, among others.

- Advertise in minority student association publications

- Participate in/host minority student job fairs

- Sponsor minority student association events

- Firm's professionals participate on career panels at school

- Outreach to leadership of minority student organizations

- Scholarships or intern/fellowships for minority students

- Sponsor, in the past, of Lesbian, Gay, Bisexual and Transgender student group conferences

Professional Recruiting

What activities does the firm undertake to attract women and minorities?

- Partner programs with women and minority banking associations
- Conferences: numerous events throughout the year at national and regional levels
- Participate at minority job fairs: HACE, ALPFA, National Black MBA, National Society of Hispanic MBAs, Toigo, The Consortium, UFSC, COPD, among others.
- Actively involved in the Forte Foundation
- Seek referrals from other professionals
- Utilize online job services

Do you use executive recruiting/search firms to seek to identify new diversity hires? Yes

If yes, list all women- and/or minority-owned executive search/recruiting firms to which the firm paid a fee for placement services in the past 12 months:
Through our Supplier Diversity Network, we work with a wide variety of executive search firms to assist us in our diversity recruiting efforts.

Internships

JPMorgan Chase has over 15 different summer internship programs, all of which hire a significant number of diverse candidates. Those divisions hiring interns include everything from Technology and Credit Card Services to Investment Banking and Human Resources. Summer interns are given a large amount of responsibility and are expected to become integral members of their teams over the 10 week summer program.

In order to supplement our on-campus recruiting efforts, we work closely with SEO, INROADS, HSF and HACU to source diverse talent for our many summer programs. Deadlines vary for the internships, but most are in January and February with interviews taking place in February and March. The pay also varies across the different lines of business within the bank and is competitive with the salaries paid by other financial services firms. The percentage of interns receiving offers of full-time employment varies from year to year, but is generally a very high percentage.

Scholarships

The JPMorgan Chase UNCF Scholars Program is dedicated to finding undergraduate students who have a commitment to diversity. The program is open to all students, regardless of race or ethnicity, but the common factors are that all applicants must have a commitment to diversity, high academic achievement and leadership qualities. Each year we select up to 20 students to join the program who each receive up to $10,000 in scholarship money in addition to a guaranteed summer internship. Students apply through the UNCF website at: www.uncf.org/internships/internshipdetail.asp?Sch_ID=296

Applications for the academic year 2005-06 will be accepted beginning over the summer 2005 through mid-November 2005. Students can apply when they are in their sophomore or junior years. Students from any and all schools can apply – the program is not limited to students from UNCF schools. JPMorgan Chase has simply engaged UNCF to help administer the program. Consequently, students of all races from all four-year colleges are encouraged to apply.

Affinity Groups/Employee Networks

Below is a listing and short description of the many affinity groups at JPMorgan Chase.

Access Ability
Access Ability is a resource on disability issues, a voice for employees with disabilities and an active partner in the success of JPMorgan Chase.

Adelante
Adelante is an employee networking group that promotes the development of Latino/Hispanic employees within JPMorgan Chase.

Administrative Professionals Network (APN)
The Administrative Professionals Network (APN) is an information and development forum for administrative staff at JPMorgan Chase.

Administrators Network Team (ANT)
The Administrators Network Team is a London-based Employee Networking Group where members provide a supportive network for one another.

AsPIRE
AsPIRE is an Employee Networking Group that enhances the professional development and leadership opportunities for JPMorgan Chase employees of Asian/Pacific Islander heritage.

BRAVO
The Bravo! Employee Networking Group is made up of employees from various backgrounds within JPMorgan Chase joining together to promote and celebrate the Italian culture and history.

Cultural Exchange (Ohio)
The Cultural Exchange is the umbrella organization for seven employee networking groups in Columbus, Ohio: Adelante, AsPIRE, N.A.T.I.O.N.S., PRIDE, ujima, Women of Color Connections and Women's Network.

Experienced Professionals Network (EPN)
EPN is an employee networking group that promotes an environment where the knowledge, skills and wisdom of the company's over-forty population are recognized, valued and leveraged.

Flexible Initiatives Network (FLING)
FLING is committed to creating a successful flexible work environment at JPMorgan Chase.

LINK (Louisiana Inclusive Networking Krewe)
LINK is an Employee Networking Group in Louisiana for employees from all backgrounds and all Lines of Businesses, who have come together to form a networking representing a broad range of experiences.

Men Aligning Together to Expand Resources (MATTER)
MATTER provides unity and support in areas of community outreach, mentoring and development, and networking and teamwork.

Native American Tribes Instilling Opportunities and Network Support (N.A.T.I.O.N.S.)
A combination of Native American and non-Native American JPMorgan Chase employees working together to support diversity by improving opportunities for group members and providing a sense of openness and inclusiveness.

Parents Networking Group (PNG)
The Parents Network is an employee networking group based in Europe/Middle East/Africa. Its mission is to provide working parents with the opportunity to succeed in balancing family and career at JPMorgan.

PRIDE
PRIDE is an employee resource network seeking to support workplace fairness for Lesbian, Gay, Bisexual and Transgender (LGBT) employees, working to consistently enhance an inclusive work environment and encouraging career growth opportunities. PRIDE is open to all JPMorgan Chase employees, regardless of sexual orientation or gender identity.

Professional Networking Association (PNA)
PNA is an employee networking group of enthusiastic, motivated, and outgoing young and young-minded professionals who want to share knowledge and ideas about their professional and personal development.

Society for Learning & Advancement of Irish-American Networking Through Experience (SLAINTE)

SLAINTE is an employee networking group comprised of over 300 employees with the goal of leveraging cultural ties to encourage employee networking, while facilitating the cultural development of our members through participation in traditional Irish customs, as well as philanthropy through a global charity based in Ireland.

South Asian Society (SAS)

This London-based Employee Networking Group looks to maximize the impact of South Asians in making JPMorgan Chase the most successful financial services institution in the world.

Ujima

Ujima is an employee networking group to provide a forum for JPMorgan Chase employees of African descent.

Women of Color Connections (WOCC)

WOCC is an employee networking group for women of color designed to promote awareness of the unique challenges associated with the WOC experience.

Women's Network @ JPMorgan Chase (WIN)

The WIN Employee Networking Group provides a forum for the company's women to collaborate and grow as professionals.

Working Families Network (WFN)

Formerly the Working Parents Network (WPN), Working Families is an Employee Networking Group comprised of JPMorgan Chase colleagues whose primary purpose is to give working parents opportunities to succeed in balancing family and career at JPMorgan Chase.

Entry-level Programs/Full-time Opportunities/Training Programs

JPMorgan Chase has 16 different entry-level full-time programs for BAs. They are as follows:

- Information Technology
- Internal Consulting Services
- Operations Management
- Finance & Accounting

- Credit Card Services
- Retail Financial Services
- In-Store Sales Management
- Corporate Finance
- Public Finance
- Equity Sales & Trading
- Fixed Income Sales & Trading
- Equity Research
- Fixed Income Research
- Private Banking
- Investment Management
- Commercial Banking

A very large number of the annual hires into these programs come from the summer intern programs. The rest of the candidates are hired through the on-campus recruiting process and through referrals and resume drops. The recruiting process takes place in the fall of the student's senior year. Resume deadlines vary, but most of the programs require resumes to be submitted in late September/early October. Interviews then take place in mid to late October and go into November. Virtually all of the hiring is complete by the end of December, though a few of the programs continue their hiring process into the spring semester.

Training varies from program to program, but in all cases it is extensive and provides the newly hired BAs with a full complement of tools and skills to bring to the job. Some programs train for a few weeks, others train for a few months. In addition, the bank offers literally hundreds of on-line and in-person courses each month across the bank on many different topics and skill-building exercises. Employees are also able to take work-related classes at colleges and universities after work and on the weekend and be reimbursed for the tuition costs of those courses up to a certain total for the year (depending on if the classes are at the BA or Masters level.)

With the advent of the JPMorgan and Bank One merger, our business footprint around the country has expanded dramatically. Consequently, there are full-time positions for BA graduates in New York, Chicago, San Francisco, Los Angeles, Columbus, Dallas, Houston, Phoenix, Detroit, Boston and Wilmington, DE. In addition, there are spots available in other cities in states around the country including New Jersey, Ohio, Connecticut, Illinois, Arizona, Michigan and Texas.

At the careers portion of our website you can learn more about the specific programs: careers.jpmorganchase.com/ba-main.html

In addition to opportunities in the U.S., there are many jobs in London, Tokyo and Hong Kong for BA graduates. Those jobs, though, are generally taken by nationals from those countries. So, for instance, if you are a European student attending school in the U.S. and you would like to work in London, you can apply for jobs at the "Europe" link on our careers website.

Diversity Mission Statement

We want to attract the best talent in the industry. To meet this goal, we are creating a workplace where differences are respected. Gender, race, sexual orientation, age and physical ability are just some of the differences that make people unique as individuals and give us the diversity of experience and perspective that make us stronger.

Additional Information

What makes JPMorgan Chase "best practice"
All of us at JPMorgan Chase are strongly committed to making diversity an integral part of how we manage and do business. When we embarked upon our formal diversity program several years ago we knew that, to be successful, our efforts had to be central to our management processes and our business practices. It's this fact that diversity is closely woven into every aspect of our culture that makes our programs so unique. Specifically, we believe our diversity efforts could be considered "best practice" as follows:

- Senior management accountability. All JPMorgan Chase senior managers are held accountable for managing to a formal diversity plan and for linking diversity to education, recruiting, succession planning, career development and business growth. No leadership positions at JPMorgan Chase are filled without at least one person of color and two women on the candidate slate.

- Senior management involvement. In addition to the company-wide JPMorgan Chase Diversity Council led by Chairman and CEO Bill Harrison, each line of business hosts its own diversity council chaired by its respective business executive, thus ensuring hands-on employee involvement in our diversity initiatives. We now have 50 diversity councils around the world, involving some

1,400 employees, and more than 90 employee networking group chapters involving 20,000 employees.

- Our supplier diversity efforts significantly contribute to the overall success of JPMorgan Chase. We understand the value of having a diverse supplier portfolio and are a recognized market leader in Supplier Diversity. Since 1994, the company has spent over $3.4 billion with over 1000 diverse businesses. Our Supplier Diversity efforts assist diverse suppliers in realizing economic growth and development. We believe that by helping to build a strong and vibrant business community through the utilization and development of certified diverse businesses, we create mutually beneficial business relationships.

- Extending the concept of diversity. We're at the forefront of extending the focus of our diversity efforts beyond race and gender. Our education efforts and dialogue with JPMorgan Chase employees are inclusive of everything that makes us unique as individuals – including race, gender, disabilities, religion, sexual orientation and age.

- Supporting work-life balance. No other US employer is involved in an effort such as JPMorgan Chase's aggressive construction plan for back-up childcare centers. We believe we need to support the diverse work-life needs of our employees and, as a result, have a network of 16 on-site childcare centers in major JPMorgan Chase sites across the US.

At Lehman Brothers, we do ground-breaking deals.
Recruiting you, for instance.

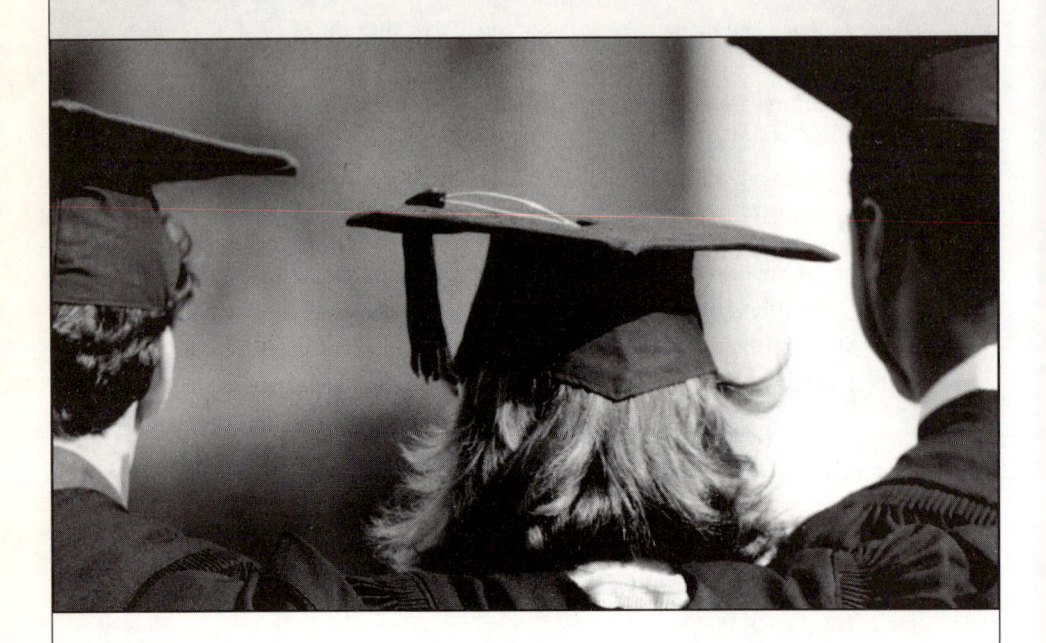

At Lehman Brothers, our greatest investment is in our human capital.
We hire smarter — and have earned a reputation for targeting
high-potential men and women.
And we train smarter, too — offering one of the most intensive
training and development programs in the industry.

To learn more, visit us online at www.lehman.com/careers

LEHMAN BROTHERS
Where vision gets built.

Lehman Brothers is an EOE. ©2005 Lehman Brothers Inc. All rights reserved. Member SIPC.

Lehman Brothers

745 Seventh Avenue
New York, NY 10019
www.lehman.com/careers

Locations

New York, NY (HQ)
America, Europe, Asia

The Stats

Revenue (2004): $11.6 billion (U.S.)
Revenue (2004): $19.6 billion (Worldwide)

Contact Information

Contact Person: Anne Erni, Managing Director, Chief Diversity Officer Diversity Team Leader/Diversity

Campus Recruiting Team Leader: Deirdre O'Donnell, Senior Vice President, Global Head of Diversity Recruiting

Lateral Recruiting Team Leader: Erica Irish Brown, Senior Vice President

Diversity URL: www.lehman.com/who/diversity/

Strategic Plan and Diversity Leadership

How does the firm's leadership communicate the importance of diversity to everyone at the firm?
Leadership communication related to diversity utilizes all avenues available within the firm, including Divisional Town Hall meetings, e-mails to all employees from senior leaders, postings to the firm's intranet (known as LehmanLive), the Lehman Daily News (a broadcast email to highlight news impacting the entire firm), event invitations, periodic Diversity Newsletters, Recruiting Updates, brochures, posters in elevators and floor lobbies.

Who has primary responsibility for leading overall diversity initiatives at your firm?
Anne Erni, Managing Director and Chief Diversity Officer

Who has primary responsibility for diversity recruiting initiatives at your firm, if different from?

Deirdre O'Donnell, Senior Vice President and Global Head of Diversity Recruiting
Erica Irish Brown, Senior Vice President

Does your firm currently have a diversity committee? No

If yes, does the committee's representation include one or more members of the firm's management/executive committee (or the equivalent)? Yes
The firm does not currently have a corporate-wide diversity council, however there are regional and divisional councils chaired by their respective business leaders. The following committees are currently active: European Regional Diversity Committee, Equities Divisional Diversity Committee, and Operations Divisional Diversity Committee.

If yes, how many senior managers are on the committee, and how often did the committee convene in furtherance of the firm's diversity initiatives in 2004?
There are approximately 15 to 18 members in each of the regional and divisional diversity councils, all of whom are Senior Vice Presidents or Managing Directors.

Total senior managers on committee: 48
Number of diversity meetings annually: The councils meet on average 8 to 10 times during the year.

Does the committee(s) and/or diversity leader establish and set goals or objectives consistent with management's priorities? Yes

Has the firm undertaken a formal or informal diversity program or set of initiatives aimed at increasing the diversity of the firm? Yes, formal

How often does the firm's management review the firm's diversity progress/results? Twice a year

How are the firm's diversity committee(s) and/or firm management held accountable for achieving results?
Lehman Brothers holds all management, including those at the top of the organization, accountable for diversity. Each business division is responsible for developing an annual diversity plan which addresses their particular opportunities and defines measurable action steps for achieving results. Regional CEOs and the firm's president review the diversity plans. To the extent a division is successful in achieving their diversity goals, they are rewarded with an additional pool of incentive compensation to allocate to employees who have made a significant contribution to the divisional diversity effort. Our performance management system incorporates criteria on diversity practices for all employees.

Are the members of the diversity committee or committees involved in diversity activities?
Executive Sponsorship is a key component of Lehman Brothers' diversity strategy. Members of the firm's Executive Committee work with each of the employee networks. Through their involvement, they champion the networks' efforts in recruiting, education and awareness initiatives. Examples include:

- Chairman and CEO Dick Fuld addressing audiences at major Women's Initiatives Leading Lehman (WILL) events
- Jasjit Bhattal, Executive Committee Member and CEO of Lehman Brothers
- Asia, addressing an audience during an Asian Leadership Speaker Series
- Hosted by Lehman Brothers Asian Network (LBAN)
- Steve Lessing, Executive Committee Member taking part in a number of The Latin American Council (TLAC) events and hosting the year-end reception

Recruitment of New Analysts and Associates

On-campus

Please list the schools at which your firm recruits.

- *Ivy League schools:* Harvard (AN/AS), Yale (AN/AS), Princeton (AN), Cornell (AN/AS), Columbia (AN/AS), Brown (AN), Penn (AN/AS), Dartmouth (AN/AS)

- *Public state schools:* UCLA (AN/AS), UT-Austin (AN/AS), UMichigan (AS), UNC (AS), UVA (AN/AS)

- *Private schools:* Amherst, Northwestern (AN/AS), Stanford (AN/AS), Williams, Duke (AN/AS), Georgetown, Johns Hopkins, NYU (AN/AS), Wesleyan, MIT (AN/AS), UChicago (AS)

- *Historically Black Colleges and Universities (HBCUs):* Morehouse, Spelman

- *Women's colleges:* Wellesley, Smith, Mt. Holyoke, Bryn Mawr, Barnard

In addition to the schools listed above, Lehman Brothers hires many students from other schools through its targeted recruiting program, which focuses on reaching out to strong candidates from universities across the country into our analyst programs.

Of the schools that you listed above, do you have any special outreach efforts directed to encourage minority students to consider your firm?

- Hold a reception for minority students
- Conferences: NBMBAA, NSHMBA, Reaching Out Conference, MBA Jumpstart, SHPE, NSBE
- Advertise in minority student association publication(s)
- Participate in/host minority student job fair(s)
- Sponsor minority student association events
- Firm's professionals participate on career panels at school
- Outreach to leadership of minority student organizations
- Scholarships or intern/fellowships for minority students
- Resume and Interview Skills Workshops

Professional Recruiting

What activities does the firm undertake to attract women and minorities?
All of the firm's diversity initiatives are aimed at attracting, hiring and retaining qualified diverse candidates and employees. In 2005, the firm hired a full-time diversity lateral recruitment team that concentrates solely on identifying top female and minority candidates for new job openings. The group's primary focus is hiring individuals into front office positions at the vice-president level and above.

All internal recruiters assist hiring managers in sourcing diverse candidates through various professional and charitable organizations, organization and job posting websites, conferences and other contacts. These resources include the Financial Women's Association, 85 Broads, Toigo Foundation, LatPro.com, America's Job Bank, Hot Jobs and alumni networks such as Columbia Business School's African American Alumni Association. Hiring managers are encouraged to post all new openings internally and externally for all employees and others to have the opportunity to apply and to ensure that there is a diverse slate of qualified candidates for open positions before extending an offer. In addition, the firm offers a training program entitled, "Interviewing through a Diversity Lens," which helps hiring managers identify the difference between preferences and requirements and enables them to be more objective during the recruiting and interviewing process.

In addition to campus recruiting, the lateral recruiting team attends annual conferences for the National Black MBA Association, the National Society of Hispanic MBAs and the Association of Latino Professionals in Finance and Accounting as well as the National Association of Securities Professionals (NASP). Lehman participates in various professional career fairs including the Annual Asian Diversity Career Expo, the NY/ NJ Metro Diversity Career Fair sponsored by the National Society of Hispanic MBAs, the National Association of African Americans in Human Resources (NAAAHR), the National Black MBA Association (NBMBAA) and WorkplaceDiversity.com, the Hispanic Alliance for Career Enhancement (HACE), Women for Hire, and The Toigo Foundation Annual Career Fair for Fellows and Alumni.

In addition to the external sources of candidates mentioned above, employee referrals for lateral professional hires are actively solicited from the firm's employee networks: Women's Initiatives Leading Lehman, Lehman Employees of African Descent, The Latin American Council, Lehman Brothers Asian Network and Lehman Brothers Gay and Lesbian Network.

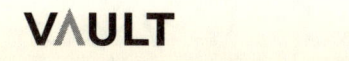

The firm requires search firms to provide hiring managers with diverse slates for each and every job opening on which they are retained. This policy is reinforced by the firm's annual "search firm breakfast," where senior management reiterates the firm's commitment to diversity and the need for search firms who wish to do business with Lehman Brothers to be equally committed.

Internships

Equities & Fixed Income Summer Analyst Program

Pay: Competitive
Length of the program: 10 weeks
Program web site: www.lehman.com\careers

The 10-week summer analyst program provides college juniors with an internship position in one of the Fixed Income Sales, Trading, Origination or Research areas, and in one of the Equity Sales, Trading or Research areas. Analysts are assigned mentors to provide guidance throughout the summer. Weekly workshops and seminars are provided to expose Interns to all areas of the firm.

The divisions look upon the summer analyst program as a primary source for hiring full-time analysts. Accordingly, those who are interested in full-time employment are strongly encouraged to apply to the summer program.

Investment Banking Summer Analyst

Pay: Competitive
Length of the program: 10 weeks
Program web site: www.lehman.com\careers

The summer analyst program provides students in the summer prior to their senior year with a chance to evaluate the working environment and career opportunities at Lehman Brothers.

The summer program begins with one week of training followed by nine weeks working in an industry, product or geographic group. Analysts are given hands-on opportunities to work as full members of client teams on a variety of transactions. They are exposed to everything a first-year analyst would experience.

Each summer analyst is assigned a senior and junior mentor to help guide him or her through their experience at Lehman Brothers. Summer analysts are provided with detailed feedback midway through and at the end of the 10-week program. They enjoy extensive contact with the firm's professionals at all levels through group events and informal functions. This invaluable experience prepares many of the summer analysts for permanent job offers in the Investment Banking Division.

The Division looks upon the summer analyst program as a primary source for hiring full-time analysts. Accordingly, those who are interested in full-time employment are strongly encouraged to apply to the summer program.

Finance Summer Analyst Program

Pay: Competitive
Length of the program: 10 weeks
Program web site: www.lehman.com\careers

Summer analysts work in the Finance Division for 10 weeks. The Finance Division offers opportunities to summer analysts in all of its major departments. These include Financial Control and Analysis, Treasury and Tax. Precise positions are determined based on business needs at the time of hire. For the most part, summer analyst positions are based on analyst program rotations, which in turn reflect entry-level positions for high potential employees. Summer analysts work with senior managers on a daily basis.

The summer analyst program also provides training to include an introductory course in global capital markets, internal faculty courses, online PC training and a weekly seminar on the different departments within the Finance Division. Summer analysts will also be asked to give weekly presentations on their work content, as well as give a group presentation at the end of the summer. Since the division looks upon the summer analyst program as a primary source for hiring full-time analysts, those who are interested in full-time employment are strongly encouraged to apply to the program.

Operations Summer Analyst Program

Pay: Competitive
Length of the program: 10 weeks
Program Web site: www.lehman.com\careers

Summer analysts are assigned to a specific business area within the Operations Division for the duration of the 10-week program. To ensure analysts receive overall exposure to the division, they are provided with a comprehensive curriculum to supplement their on-the-job experience. This curriculum includes weekly management-led overviews, presentations by internal and external experts on various financial products and market topics, and tours of the various exchanges and the Federal Reserve Bank.

The Operations Division utilizes the summer analyst program as the primary recruitment source for the full-time analyst program. Individuals who are interested in pursuing a career in the Operations Division upon graduation are strongly encouraged to apply for this program during their junior year.

Information Technology Summer Analyst Program

Pay: Competitive
Length of the program: 10 weeks
Program Web site: www.lehman.com\careers

The Information Technology Division offers a 10-week work experience program to computer science, computer/electrical engineering and information systems students entering their senior year (students in other majors with a strong technical background will also be considered).

IT summer analysts gain valuable experience and knowledge while meeting new people and learning new skills. Training and a weekly speaker series featuring the Chief Information Officer and senior IT professionals provide exposure to senior management and the business of Wall Street.

In addition, the summer program can provide an opening to a full-time position and a meaningful long-term career with the firm.

Investment Management Summer Analyst Program

Pay: Competitive
Length of the program: 10 weeks
Program web site: www.lehman.com\careers

The summer analyst program provides students in the summer prior to their senior year a chance to evaluate the working environment at Lehman Brothers.

The summer analyst program is a 10-week program where each participant is provided with the chance to work in one or two different business areas. Summer analysts are given hands-on opportunities to work as full team members and are exposed to the typical work flow of a first-year analyst.

Summer analysts are provided with detailed feedback midway through and at the end of the 10-week program. They enjoy extensive contact with the firm's professionals at all levels through group events and informal functions. This invaluable experience prepares many of the summer analysts for permanent job offers in the Investment Management Division.

The Investment Management Division looks upon the summer analyst program as a primary source for hiring full-time analysts. Accordingly, those who are interested in full-time employment are strongly encouraged to apply to the summer program.

Affinity Groups/Employee Networks

Lehman Brothers' diversity initiative is aimed at attracting the best people and providing a culture and work environment that helps maximize the productivity and growth potential of each employee. Additionally, we recognize that having a diverse workforce encourages increased creativity and innovation, which are crucial drivers for continued business success. To help achieve our diversity goals, the firm endorses employee networks. In the U.S., Europe and Asia there is active participation in one or more of the following networks:

- Lehman Brothers Asian Network (LBAN)
- Lehman Brothers Gay & Lesbian Network (LBGLN)
- Lehman Employees of African Descent (LEAD)
- The Latin American Council (TLAC)
- Women's Initiatives Leading Lehman (WILL)
- Disability Working Forum

Entry-level Programs/Full-time Opportunities/Training Programs

Equities & Fixed Income Analyst Program

Length of program: Two to three years
Geographic location(s) of program: New York

The two- to three-year program begins in New York with several weeks of classroom training in which all Sales, Trading & Research Training (START) analysts participate. The training consists of an orientation to the firm and a comprehensive capital markets course covering a variety of topics, including stock and bond analysis as well as an overview of all the major capital markets instruments and businesses. Analysts gain exposure to many aspects of the firm through a series of business presentations, lectures and interactive projects. Additionally, analysts receive training for the Series 7 and Series 63 licensing exams.

At the completion of the training program, generalist analysts will begin a rotation process through our Equities and Fixed Income Divisions. Analysts will have the opportunity to explore various areas and roles, and will have the ability to state their placement preferences following these intensive interactions. Placement decisions are made by the global heads of both the Equities and Fixed Income Divisions at the end of the rotation process and are based on the overall business needs and analyst preferences.

Investment Banking Analyst Program

Length of program: Two to three years
Geographic location(s) of program: New York, Los Angeles, Menlo Park, Chicago, Houston

All analysts begin their two- to three-year program with a four-week training program in New York. This training introduces them to the firm and its team-oriented approach and reinforces the skills that they will apply as investment bankers.

Classroom training during the first four weeks includes technical skills training in accounting, computer modeling and financial valuation techniques. The incoming analysts also participate in small teams on projects which provide them with a better understanding of the firm's capabilities and enable them to develop a global network of peers.

Following the classroom training, analysts return to their region of hire and join one of the firm's industry, product or regionally-focused groups. This placement is based on the particular interest of the analyst and on the firm's needs. Each analyst participates as a fully contributing member of selected project teams, working with bankers at all levels on diverse assignments.

Investment Management Analyst Program

Length of program: Two to three years
Geographic location(s) of program: New York

The two- to three-year analyst program begins with an orientation to the firm and classroom training. The training program includes a comprehensive capital markets course that covers a variety of topics, including stock and bond analysis as well as an overview of the major capital markets instruments and businesses. During this training program, our analysts will gain exposure to many aspects of the firm through a series of business presentations, lectures and interactive projects. Following the capital markets module, our analysts receive in-depth training on our Investment Management Division's platform, products and capabilities. In addition, analysts will receive training for the Series 7 and Series 63 registration exams.

Investment Management Division analysts will have the opportunity to sample jobs in our different functional areas such as: Investments & Research, Client Development & Marketing and New Product Development & Strategy. Permanent placement decisions are made based on the overall business needs and analyst preferences.

Operations Analyst Program

Length of program: Two years
Geographic location(s) of program: New York, New Jersey

The two-year program begins with a three-day orientation hosted by the senior management of the Operations Division. At the conclusion of the orientation, analysts are placed throughout the division based on business needs.

Analysts receive comprehensive on-the-job training, which is supplemented with web-based and instructor-led programs.

After one year of successful performance within their initial placement, analysts are eligible to explore available opportunities within the division.

Finance Analyst Program

Length of program: Two years
Geographic location(s) of program: New York

The Finance analyst program is a two-year rotational program. Analysts undertake three successive eight-month rotations in various departments of the Finance Division, including Financial Control and Analysis, Treasury and Tax. The rotational structure of the program exposes analysts to a broad range of functions and departments within the Finance Division and allows them to gain experience with capital markets products and to build financial skills. As a result, the program allows analysts to develop their interests as they are prepared for careers in management roles.

Information Technology Analyst Program

Geographic location(s) of program: New York

The Technology Development Program is an intensive four-month training program that includes technical training, financial markets instruction, professional development and leadership skills guidance and a speaker series led by senior management in the IT Division.

The interview process and subsequent job placements are made based on the individual's background, skills, experience and interest. Technical training is then customized based on the individual's placement.

Diversity Mission Statement

Chairman and Chief Executive Officer, Richard S. Fuld, Jr. has made the following statement with regard to diversity and inclusion:

"At Lehman Brothers, diversity is an integral part of our vision and a business imperative. We define diversity as valuing differences in thought and perspective. Our goal is to integrate diversity into every aspect of our business – from dealing with our clients to managing our workforce.

Our continued success rests in our ability to be the firm of choice for the very best people from the widest available pools of talent. To this end, we are dedicating significant time and resources to promote a diverse and inclusive workplace.

- Our employee networks in the U.S. and Europe are committed to enriching our "One Firm" culture and to fostering an inclusive environment for all employees.

- Global, regional and divisional diversity councils are in place, expanding and working proactively to enhance and implement our diversity plans.

- Lehman Brothers supports a range of global sponsorships that promote diversity.

The strength of Lehman Brothers' culture has helped us to achieve wonderful success. Both our culture and our success depend on the quality and breadth of the people who are part of our firm. It is critical that our organization continue the momentum to broaden the representation of our employees – to ensure that diversity of thought and perspective is brought to our clients. At Lehman Brothers, we see diversity as good business practice."

Additional Information

At Lehman Brothers we are committed to attracting, retaining and developing the best people from the broadest backgrounds, and to nurturing our inclusive culture that fosters employee development and contributes to our commercial success.

Each of our employees comes from a unique background, each brings a diverse perspective to the firm based on his or her variety of life experiences. This variety of thought and perspective is of intrinsic value to us in our talent evaluation process.

To assist in the retention and development of our people, we emphasize tools such as networking opportunities, mentoring programs, employee and management education and training, and corporate citizenship.

Following are a sample of our employee programs:

- Employee Networks in all geographic regions open to all employees

- Over 500 employees act as mentors in one of over 20 mentoring programs

- Over 10,000 employees have taken part in our Awareness Training program, with more slated before the end of the year

- The firm and its networks partnered with over 70 diversity related community organizations in 2004, either through financial or volunteer sponsorship. These include:

- Student organizations: SEO, Robert A. Toigo, Posse, Capital Chances, Opportunity Now

- Community organizations: Robin Hood, Harlem's Children Zone, Girl Scouts

- Professional organizations: New York Women's Foundation, National Association of Asian Professionals, The Hispanic Federation, The Twenty First Century Foundation

Life balance

Investment Banking is characterized by fast-paced, demanding work environments; however, Lehman is highly committed to fostering a culture that supports and respects our employees' need to balance the complex and sometimes competing demands of their careers and personal lives.

Our enhanced policies and benefits reflect our commitment to this culture; resources are dedicated specifically to ensuring we maintain best practices.

Our most recent policy enhancements took place in 2004, and included:

- An extra week of paid vacation for nearly all employees

- Implementation of firm-sponsored flexible work arrangements including reduced or compressed work week, flextime, and telecommuting or flexspace for employees with conducive roles

- Introduction of a partially-paid sabbatical for tenured employees

- Increased subsidies for adoption, additional time off for elder care, bereavement and secondary care givers after childbirth or adoption.

All these policies reinforce the value we place on contributions and results versus face time.

Career mobility is also emphasized through the firm's support of internal transfers; managers are encouraged to fill staffing vacancies through the transfer or promotion of current employees of the firm, whenever possible.

Recognition of our efforts

Selected achievements in 2004:

- Opportunity Now Focus Group Award for strategy and commitment to diversity and inclusion in the U.K.

- 100% on the Human Rights Campaign's* Corporate Equality Index for the past two years

- America's largest gay, lesbian, bisexual and transgender organization

- Top 40 "Ideal Diversity Employers" in the Black Collegian/Universum campus survey (both M.B.A. and undergraduate students)

- "Dr. Antonia Pantoja Corporate Leadership Award" by Aspira of New York for leadership and support of Hispanic youth

Thank you so much for you interest in Lehman Brothers. We are proud of our commitment to diversity and inclusion, and wish you good fortune in your career aspirations.

YOU COULD REACH FOR THE MOON.

BUT WHY STOP THERE?

Stars, like people, have differences. But what they do have in common are energy, fire, brilliance - and limitless possibilities.

Merrill Lynch is proud to be a firm that offers exceptional people everywhere their opportunity to shine. By encouraging collaboration between people of different backgrounds and expertise, we're able to create smarter solutions for clients — and put our firm at the very center of the financial universe.

Consider this your invitation to be brilliant with us.

Merrill Lynch
ml.com/careers
ml.com/about/diversity

EXCEPTIONAL *WITHOUT EXCEPTION*
Merrill Lynch is an equal opportunity employer.

Merrill Lynch & Co.

World Financial Center
New York, NY 10080
Phone: 212-449-1000
www.ml.com

Locations

New York, NY (HQ)
Other locations in the U.S., Europe, Middle East & Africa, Pacific Rim, Canada, & Latin America

The Stats

Revenue (2004): $15.878 billion (U.S.)
Revenue (2004): $22 billion (Worldwide)

Contact Information

Contact Person: Keith Webb, Director, Undergraduate Diversity Recruiter, Merrill Lynch
Campus Recruiting Team Leader: Elizabeth Wamai, Director, Diversity Manager, Merrill Lynch
Diversity URL: ml.com/aboutdiversity

Strategic Plan and Diversity Leadership

How does the firm's leadership communicate the importance of diversity to everyone at the firm?
E-mails, newsletters, town halls, quarterly meetings, bulletin, etc.

Who has primary responsibility for leading overall diversity initiatives at your firm?
The CEO. Additionally, the Chief Administrative Officer, Heads of Businesses, the President of Global Private Client and the Co-President of Global Markets and Investment Banking serve as co-chairs of the Diversity Employee Advisory Council.

Who has primary responsibility for diversity recruiting initiatives at your firm?
Global Head of Campus Recruiting and the Director of Diversity Recruiting

Does your firm currently have a diversity committee? Yes

If yes, does the committee's representation include one or more members of the firm's management/executive committee (or the equivalent)? Yes

How many senior managers are on the committee, and how often did the committee convene in furtherance of the firm's diversity initiatives in 2004?
There are 21 senior managers on the committee from across various businesses. The co-chairs sit on the firm's executive operating committee. The committee met four times in 2004.

> *Total senior managers on committee:* 25 (including co-chairs)
> *Number of diversity meetings annually:* 4 meetings annually, 2 of those with the External Diversity Advisory Board

If you have more than one diversity committee, please list.
We have an External Diversity Advisory Board which is comprised of five distinguished leaders who bring special expertise, perspective and experience to our workforce diversity efforts. They work with management and the Diversity Employee Advisory Council to share ideas about the recruitment, retention and development of diverse talent as well as business development in diverse markets.

Does the committee(s) and/or diversity leader establish and set goals or objectives consistent with management's priorities? Yes

Has the firm undertaken a formal or informal diversity program or set of initiatives aimed at increasing the diversity of the firm? Yes, formal and informal

How often does the firm's management review the firm's diversity progress/results? Quarterly

How is the firm's diversity committee(s) and/or firm management held accountable for achieving results?
The firm is held accountable by the main ML Board of Directors and reports regularly to the Board on diversity related matters.

Are the members of the diversity committee or committees involved in diversity activities? Yes

If so, list and describe some of those activities.

Among some of the activities they are aligned and involved with are: business development initiatives in diverse communities, recruitment and retention, communications and branding, and employee networks.

Recruitment of New Analysts and Associates

On-campus

Please list the schools at which your firm recruits.

ML recruits at all the below types of institutions, and also at education-based non-profit organizations that recruit/work with diverse students, e.g. SEO, INROADS, Inner City Scholarship Fund, Jackie Robinson Foundation, LEAD Program in Business Alumni.

- Ivy League schools
- Public state schools
- Private schools
- Historically Black Colleges and Universities (HBCUs)
- Hispanic Serving Institutions (HSIs)
- Native American Tribal Universities
- Other predominantly minority and/or women's colleges

Of the schools that you listed above, are there any special outreach efforts directed to encourage minority students to consider your firm?

- Hold a reception for minority students
- Conferences: DISCO, NAFEO, UNCF, Native Ivy League Conference
- Advertise in minority student association publications
- Participate in/host minority student job fairs
- Sponsor minority student association events
- Firm's professionals participate on career panels at schools
- Outreach to leadership of minority student organizations
- Scholarships or intern/fellowships for minority students
- Host/sponsor Merrill Lynch-specific events for women and minority students

Professional Recruiting

What activities does the firm undertake to attract women and minorities?

- Partner programs with women and minority banking associations
- Conferences: NBMBAA, NSHMBAA, AIRS Diversity Conference, Wall Street Journal Diversity Conference for Executives, NABA, ALPFA
- Participate at minority job fairs
- Seek referrals from other professionals
- Utilize online job services
- Host and sponsor diversity-specific programs and initiatives targeted to women and minorities

Do you use executive recruiting/search firms to seek to identify new diversity hires? Yes

Internships

Merrill Lynch has summer analyst programs in the following businesses:

- Investment Banking
- Global Equity and Global Debt Markets
- Equity and Debt Research
- Private Client

- Merrill Lynch Investment Managers
- Credit
- Operations
- Technology
- Accounting and Finance
- Human Resources

The following program participants are involved in the above programs:

- SEO Program
- INROADS

Deadline for application for the internship: Deadlines vary but students should go to ml.com/careers for specific program deadlines.

Length of the program: 10 weeks for all programs including approximately one week of training

Percentage of interns in the program who receive offers of full-time employment: We have a high conversion rate. Most of our interns receive offers to return full-time or, if they are sophomores or freshmen, offers to return the following summer.

Web site for internship information: ml.com/careers

Please describe the internship program, including departments hiring, intern responsibilities, qualifications for the program and any other details you feel are relevant.

Please visit the website for detailed summer internship descriptions: ml.com/careers

Scholarships

Name of scholarship program: ML offers various scholarships to sophomores and juniors, at a variety of institutions, including HBCUs.

Deadline for application for the scholarship program: Deadlines vary from January to February

Scholarship award amount: Ranges from $5,000 to $10,000

Web site or other contact information for scholarship: ml.com/careers

Please describe the scholarship program, including basic requirements, eligibility, length of program and any other details you feel are relevant.

The main requirement is that the scholarship recipient receives and accepts a summer intern position at ML.

Affinity Groups/Employee Networks

Merrill Lynch has eight global employee affinity groups called Employee Professional Networks. These are:

- Women's Network
- Black Professional Network
- Hispanic Professional Network
- Asian-Pacific American Professional Network
- Indo-American Professional Network
- Rainbow Professional Network
- Disability Professional Network
- Native American Professional Network

The Employee Professional Networks are employee-led local networks, organized regionally across and within business groups. They share a common purpose to build a robust and diverse leadership pipeline that drives profitability while promoting an understanding of Merrill Lynch's core values, corporate policies, business goals, career opportunities and philanthropic objectives.

The primary objectives of the networks include diversified business development, recruitment and retention and community leadership. They also provide a forum for Merrill Lynch employees to share experiences and professional advice that can assist them in reaching their performance potential and career aspirations.

Entry-level Programs/Full-time Opportunities/Training Programs

Merrill Lynch has full-time entry-level opportunities in the following businesses:

- Investment Banking
- Global Equity and Global Debt Markets
- Equity and Debt Research
- Private Client
- Merrill Lynch Investment Managers
- Credit
- Operations
- Technology
- Accounting and Finance
- Human Resources

These programs range from 2-3 years and include a training component at the beginning of the program. The training component varies by business area and is a combination of formal classroom instruction, assignments, social activities, and a mentor program that provides guidance and direction.

> *Length of program:* 2-3 years for entry level programs for undergraduate. This varies by program. Visit ml.com/careers to learn more.
>
> *Geographic location(s) of program:* New York, Princeton and/or Hopewell in New Jersey. For Investment Banking we have opportunities in Chicago, Houston, Los Angeles, Palo Alto and Toronto.

Additional Information

As Merrill Lynch has successfully reinvented itself over the years – from a U.S.-based retail securities broker to a diversified global financial services company – our workforce diversity efforts have evolved as well. The focus on race and gender issues that initially drove our diversity initiatives in the United States now has a global perspective. We want to ensure that Merrill Lynch is a meritocracy in which diversity thrives at every level and at every location of the company.

"Merrill Lynch really does have a unique character as an organization – we are embracing of so many people who may differ in their gender, ethnicity, place of origin or even their personal styles and political beliefs. That character is a tremendous

asset and is the foundation behind my belief that unleashing the creative energy of our people is what will enable our company to realize its full potential."

Stan O'Neal
Chairman, CEO & President

At Merrill Lynch, diversity is more than just a word or a single program – it is part of an environment in which employees are recognized and rewarded based on their accomplishments. Rooted in one of the company's five guiding principles – respect for the individual – the Merrill Lynch culture promotes mutual respect, acceptance, cooperation and productivity among people from varying backgrounds.

Morgan Stanley

195 Broadway, 19th Floor
New York, NY 10007
Phone: (917) 790-5601
www.morganstanley.com

Locations

New York, NY (HQ)
600 offices in 28 countries.

The Stats

Currently our 53,718 people represent over 120 nationalities and speak 90 languages.

Contact Information

Diversity Team Leader/Diversity Campus Recruiting Team Leader:
Nicole Griffith, Director

Diversity URL:
www.morganstanley.com/about/diversity

E-mail:
diversityrecruiting@morganstanley.com

Strategic Plan and Diversity Leadership

How does the firm's leadership communicate the importance of diversity to everyone at the firm?
The firm uses all mediums to promote our diversity recruiting efforts including web sites, brochures, videos, training, meetings, events and presentations.

Who has primary responsibility for leading overall diversity initiatives at your firm?
Marilyn Booker, Managing Director and Global Head of Diversity

Who has primary responsibility for diversity recruiting initiatives at your firm, if different from the above?
Nancy Travers, Vice President

Does your firm currently have a diversity committee? Yes

If yes, does the committee's representation include one or more members of the firm's management/executive committee (or the equivalent)? Yes

Does the committee(s) and/or diversity leader establish and set goals or objectives consistent with management's priorities?
Yes, the goals and objectives are set jointly and are consistent with management priorities.

Are the members of the diversity committee or committees involved in diversity activities?
Yes, diversity recruiting committee members are involved in mentoring, training, campus and lateral recruiting efforts.

Recruitment of New Analysts and Associates

On-campus

Please list the schools at which your firm recruits.
We recruit annually at over 65 undergraduate institutions in all of the below listed categories. Our calendar of school visits, events, career fairs and activities and is available through our campus website at Morgan Stanley.com/careers.

- Ivy League schools
- Public state schools
- Private schools
- Historically Black Colleges and Universities (HBCUs)
- Hispanic Serving Institutions (HSIs)
- Other predominantly minority and/or women's colleges

Of the schools that you listed above, do you have any special outreach efforts directed to encourage minority students to consider your firm?

- All of the below as well as "Day in the Life" programs, resume writing workshops, job shadowing, leadership training and networking events.
- Hold multiple receptions for minority students
- Attend national/local diversity conferences
- Advertise in minority student association publications
- Participate in/host minority student job fair
- Sponsor minority student association events
- Firm's professionals participate on career panels at school
- Outreach to leadership of minority student organizations
- Scholarships or intern/fellowships for minority students

Internships

Internship programs include the Morgan Stanley Fellowship, Richard B. Fisher Scholars Program, Posse, CityKids, A Better Chance, Prep for Prep as well as general summer Analyst programs. All of our full-time Analyst and junior associate programs recruit for summer Analysts.

Pay: Competitive
Length of the program: 10 weeks
Web site for internship information: www.morganstanley.com/careers

Richard B. Fisher Program (RBF)

The Morgan Stanley Richard B. Fisher Scholars Program is a competitive scholarship/internship program established in 1993 to provide outstanding minority undergraduates with a one or two-year financial award for exceptional academic achievement. The undergraduate students selected also receive the opportunity to gain exposure to the investment banking industry through a summer internship at the firm in Investment Banking, Research, Institutional Equity or Fixed Income. The Information Technology program is currently under review.

Relationship Partners: Prep for Prep, A Better Chance, Albert G. Oliver Program, American Indian College Fund and Hispanic Alliance for Career Enhancement

Juniors: (i) Financial award for exceptional academic achievement, (ii) a summer internship the summer prior to your senior year with Morgan Stanley, (iii) a meaningful relationship with one of the premier firms in the industry. Internships in Investment Banking, Fixed Income, Institutional Equity, Equity Research and Information Technology.

Sophomores: (i) Financial award for exceptional academic achievement, (ii) a summer internship the summer prior to your senior year with Morgan Stanley, (iii) a meaningful relationship with one of the premier firms in the industry. Internships in Investment Banking, Fixed Income, Institutional Equity, Equity Research and Information Technology.

Undergraduate Fellowship Scholars program

The Morgan Stanley Fellowship Program is a competitive scholarship program established in 1999 to provide outstanding minority students with (i) a financial award for exceptional academic achievement, (ii) an internship the summer before their junior year in Institutional Infrastructure Services and Financial Control Group (iii) a meaningful relationship with one of the premier firms in the industry.

Not for Profit Relationship Organizations

Prep for Prep
Web site: www.prepforprep.org/prepforprep/aboutus.asp

The mission of Prep for Prep is to identify and nurture a generation of leaders from minority group backgrounds who have the education, the skills, and the commitment to help guide this society towards a significant narrowing of the gap between the rhetoric of the American Dream and its blemished reality. As a strategy for developing leaders from minority groups, Prep for Prep seeks to identify those boys and girls who are most likely to benefit from attending academically-demanding independent schools. The Program attempts to prepare these youngsters for success at such schools and to instill in them a commitment to educational achievement as a means of developing their leadership potential. The Prep Community includes over 3,000 students and alumni/ae.

A Better Chance
Web site: www.abetterchance.org/index.html

Mission: Since the founding of A Better Chance in 1963, our mission has rested on a single goal: to substantially increase the number of well-educated minority youth capable of assuming positions of responsibility and leadership in American society. A Better Chance works with students of color in sixth grade through college to help them gain access to broader educational and career opportunities.

History: A Better Chance began in the 1960's as an innovative experiment in educational opportunity. At a time of political unrest, social idealism, and the struggle for civil rights, the Charles E. Merrill Foundation gave a grant that allowed twenty-three independent schools to respond to President John F. Kennedy's call for equal access to the nation's top schools for minority students. The schools' response: the Independent School Talent Search Program (ISTSP).

ISTSP held its first session for academically talented youngsters the summer of 1964 at Dartmouth College. Fifty young men had been accepted by college preparatory schools so long as they completed the summer program. That summer, the name of the program changed to Project ABC: A Better Chance.

We continue to honor the original promise to offer deserving students of color access to a quality education even as our membership has grown. Over 11,000 A Better Chance Scholars have graduated from Member Schools, which now extend across the country through 27 states. An overwhelming majority of alumni have gone on to graduate from competitive colleges, graduate programs, or professional schools. Our distinguished pool of A Better Chance alumni includes leaders in business, law, medicine, government, education, and the arts. We boast no less of the number of alumni who are leaders in their communities as well.

Hispanic Alliance for Career Enhancement

Web site: www.hace-usa.org/default.asp

Mission: HACE is dedicated to incubating and nurturing Latinos at all stages of the career continuum from high school to college and on to the professional years, as we seek to develop increasing numbers of successful Latino professionals and leaders.

Founded in 1982, HACE is a leading national non-profit organization dedicated to building Latino careers through the career development of Latino students and experienced professionals and recruitment programs for the acquisition of this talent by leading corporations, the government and other institutional employers.

Posse Foundation

Web site: www.possefoundation.org

The Posse Foundation identifies, recruits and selects student leaders from public high schools to form multicultural teams called "posses." These teams are then prepared, through an intensive eight-month Posse Training Program, for enrollment at top universities nationwide to pursue their academics and to help promote cross-cultural communication on campus. The Posse Program has exhibited great success over the past fourteen years, placing 721 students into top colleges and universities. These students have won over $63 million in scholarships from Posse partner universities and are persisting and graduating at close to 90% – a rate higher than the national averages at institutions of higher education. Posse currently has sites in four major cities across the United States: New York, Boston, Chicago and Los Angeles, and plans to launch a new program site in Washington, D.C. in 2004.

The focus of the program is twofold: 1) To recruit students who have extraordinary leadership ability and academic potential that might be overlooked by the traditional university selection process, and 2) To devote the resources and support necessary to allow those students to achieve personal and academic excellence, reach graduation and effect positive changes on their college campus and in their community.

Responsibility for the final selection of students is shared by both the participating universities and Posse.

The concept of a posse works for both students and college campuses and is rooted in the belief that a small, diverse group of talented students – a posse – carefully selected and trained, can serve as a catalyst for increased individual and community development. The Posse Foundation believes that as the United States becomes an increasingly multicultural society, those individuals sitting at the bargaining tables of the next century should be more representative of this rich demographic mix, that the nation's future will depend on the ability of strong leaders from diverse backgrounds to develop consensus solutions to complex social problems. One of the primary goals of the Posse Program is to train these leaders of tomorrow. To achieve this goal, The Posse Foundation establishes partnerships with select universities and works with them in three principal areas: recruitment, assessment, and retention.

Unlike traditional scholarship programs, Posse focuses on academics and leadership; it sends students to college in a team; it relies on ongoing university participation to ensure continuous improvement in the process and assessment of the student's change initiatives; it gives students the chance to succeed individually and as a group, an excellent foundation for the workplace; and it increases the graduation rate for non-traditional students

Jackie Robinson Foundation

Web site: www.jackierobinson.org

Founded in 1973 by Rachel Robinson, the Jackie Robinson Foundation is a public, not-for-profit, national organization that awards four year college scholarships to academically gifted students of color with financial need, enabling them to attend the college of their choice.

JR Scholars also participate in the Foundation's unique comprehensive support system that includes leadership development, mentoring programs and career counseling. The graduation rate is 92% – the highest among comparable programs in the country.

Support for JRF began with a grant from Unilever Home and Personal Care, NA in 1973. Since then more than 500 corporations, foundations and individuals have partnered with JRF in the effort to impact young lives.

Provides 4-year college scholarships of up to $6,000 annually to minority high school students to attend the college of their choice.

Albert G. Oliver Program

Web site: www.theoliverprogram.org/v2/index.html

The Oliver Program cultivates a new generation of leaders by providing exceptional New York City youth of African and Latin American descent with access to selective independent schools and continued support for achieving their future academic and professional goals.

SEO

Web site: www.seo-ny.org/

SEO was founded in 1963 during the height of the modern civil rights movement as a mentoring and college prep program for underprivileged high school students in New York City. The organization was based upon the conviction that all students can succeed when given access to opportunities. As more and more of SEO's students went on to college, SEO recognized that there was a need to advocate for increased opportunities for minorities in the corporate workforce. In 1980, the SEO Career Program was established to help high achieving students of color (Black, Hispanic/Latino, Asian and Native American) reach their career goals by providing internships in some of our nation's most challenging fields. Starting with Wall Street, the SEO Career Program began with 11 students placed at four investment banking firms. The Career Program now partners with more than 40 firms, offering over 300 career-blazing summer internships in the following eight areas.

- Accounting
- Asset Management
- Corporate Law
- Global Corporate Financial Leadership
- Information Technology
- Investment Banking – NY/NJ/CT
- Investment Banking – other major cities
- Management Consulting
- Philanthropy

Sponsors for Educational Opportunity is the nation's premiere summer internship program for talented students of color leading to full-time job offers. Since its inception, SEO's Career Program has placed over 3,500 Black, Hispanic/Latino, Asian and Native American students in internships that lead to opportunities in exciting and rewarding careers in the most competitive industries worldwide. Our program is featured in Princeton Review's 106 Best Internships in America, and is a gateway to the most coveted and highest paying careers. More than 80% of SEO interns receive job offers from partner firms after their internships. SEO grooms its interns to excel in the workplace and become leaders in their communities who will give back and forge a path to success for the next generation. As a direct result of the Career Program and the high performance of its interns, SEO has significantly increased the number of people of color employed on Wall Street and by major corporations nationwide.

Entry-level Programs/Full-time Opportunities/Training Programs

Since 1997, Morgan Stanley has combined the complementary skills and resources of two powerful organizations: Morgan Stanley, established in New York in 1935, and Dean Witter, established in 1924 in San Francisco. Their distinguished pedigrees encompass a record of historic firsts: in national and international expansion, in the use of technology, and in the development of new financial tools and techniques that have redefined the meaning of financial services for individual, institutional and investment banking clients

Morgan Stanley has earned a worldwide reputation for excellence in financial advice and market execution. The 54,142 members of Morgan Stanley in 28 countries connect people, ideas and capital to help our clients achieve their financial aspirations.

The talent and passion of our people is critical to our success. Together, we share a common set of values rooted in integrity and excellence. Morgan Stanley can provide a superior foundation for building a professional career – a place for people to learn, to achieve and to grow. A philosophy that balances personal lifestyles, perspectives and needs is an important part of our culture.

Joining an organization like Morgan Stanley is a growing and learning experience. The firm has created a variety of programs for undergraduates and graduates, in areas from Information Technology to Private Wealth Management. It is through there programs you can learn about the industry and the firm or find a place to begin your career.

Equity Research

The Morgan Stanley Global Equity Research team has earned a reputation as one of the dominant intellectual thought leaders on Wall Street.

Junior Associates play an essential role in assisting the Morgan Stanley Equity Research team in maintaining and enhancing our global research reputation. Individuals may be assigned to a dedicated industry team or may participate in rotations throughout the department. Early activities may include gathering and analyzing industry data to develop an industry vision; analyzing emerging trends in an industry or macro-economy; preparing comprehensive company reports; assessing relative stock valuations; and reviewing findings with respective senior team members and ultimately internal and external clients.

Information Technology

Partnering strategically with both business Units and industry-leading technology companies across the globe, Morgan Stanley Information Technology continues to redefine the way the Firm conducts business worldwide.

The IT Analyst Training Program is designed to develop highly skilled and motivated technologists who partner with our business to solve complex problems through the use of technology. Held twice a year, in February and August, the training program lasts 18 weeks. IT Analysts are recruited globally for a particular office – New York, London, Hong Kong or Tokyo – and train together in New York. During the four months of training, Analysts develop a network of colleagues in the IT division and build lasting relationships.

Fixed Income

Our Fixed Income Division plays an integral role in a 24-hour global market where billions of dollars in debt securities change hands every day.

Analysts within Morgan Stanley's Fixed Income Division are offered the unique opportunity to leverage and develop their quantitative and analytical skills as well as their interpersonal and communication skills. Following a five-week comprehensive training program, Analysts begin a two-year assignment in one of the following functions: sales, trading, research, structuring or finance. Traders, salespeople, and clients will use the research and analysis generated by Analysts to make real-time investment decisions. Analysts have constant opportunities to collaborate with more experienced colleagues and learn from senior Fixed Income professionals. Analysts are exposed to all aspects of fixed income transactions-idea generation, marketing, issuance, pricing and assessing ongoing market reaction-as they interact with salespeople, traders, capital markets and research professionals.

Institutional Equity

Morgan Stanley is a leader in the global origination, distribution and trading of equity, equity-related and equity derivative securities. Year after year, the Firm's equity sales and trading depth and excellence are put to use to ensure liquidity for, and provide sophisticated analytics to clients around the world.

The Equity and Sales Trading Analyst Program requires insightful, creative, quantitative thinkers, who have a desire to work in an exciting and challenging environment. A successful Analyst will possess a strong set of interpersonal skills, is detail-oriented and reacts quickly to ever-changing events and market conditions. The program begins with a six-week global training and development curriculum that includes three weeks of Firm-wide training with Analysts from the Institutional Securities Division and three weeks of equity product training. Analysts work closely with Morgan Stanley professionals and institutional clients. Responsibilities include working with Research Analysts, communicating Firm ideas to colleagues and clients, and working with equity traders and sales traders facilitating equity order flow.

Investment Management

With more than 30 years of global investment experience, Morgan Stanley Investment Management is one of the of the world's largest and best-known global asset managers.

Analysts in Investment Management begin their careers with Morgan Stanley working in one of three functional areas: the Global Investor Group, Sales and Marketing area or Operations. Positions may be located in New York, West Conshohocken, Oakbrook, Houston or Jersey City. Success as an Analyst at Morgan Stanley Investment Management requires a solid educational background with excellent analytical and quantitative skills. Proficiency with computers is essential. Superior communication skills are critical, as are organizational skills and attention to detail. A keen interest in global financial markets and a facility for in-depth research are important qualities for successful Investment Management professionals.

Investment Banking

Morgan Stanley is a worldwide leader in investment banking and is ranked among the top institutions in mergers and acquisitions, underwriting of equity and equity-related transactions, high-yield debt financing and corporate debt issuance. Consistently recognized for its exciting and fast-paced lifestyle, the Investment Banking Division at Morgan Stanley leads league tables and attracts a wide range of institutional clients.

Analysts have long been viewed as essential to Morgan Stanley's Investment Banking excellence. The Firm was the first on Wall Street to implement a comprehensive Analyst Program more than 30 years ago. Analysts work on a variety of assignments, from business development presentations to equity and debt offerings, mergers and acquisitions, and real estate financings. Analysts will complete a diverse array of projects, usually working on several assignments simultaneously with some of the most experienced investment bankers in the industry. As an Analyst, you will receive an introduction to financial analysis and an exposure to a variety of industries, business scenarios and financial products. You will hone your business judgment, develop an understanding of how the capital markets work and learn how to model complex financial scenarios.

Finance

The Finance Division is a service organization responsible for the guardianship of the firm's financial well-being, both at the product and overall company level.

The Infrastructure Analyst Program consists of four weeks of classroom and project-based learning to provide Analysts with business, technical and professional knowledge. Specific classes focus on the life cycle of a trade, basic product knowledge and key areas of the regulatory environment.

Corporate Treasury Analysts participate in a two- to three-week firmwide training program and receive a broad-based introduction to financial analysis, as well as exposure to all of the principal business units of an investment bank. Analysts also develop an understanding of the inner workings of a global financial services firm and a keen sense of how the capital markets work.

Credit Risk Management Analysts participate in a two- to three-week Firmwide training program, followed by additional credit-specific training. Analysts receive on-the-job learning, gaining hands-on experience in finance and accounting as well as exposure to a wide range of industries, corporate and financial institutions, and business transactions. Analysts evaluate trade counterparties, determine the credit-related implications of investment banking transactions and help to manage product-specific exposures and risk positions for Sales and Trading. Analysts also conduct due diligence investigations, interview company management and perform in-depth analyses of financial statements.

Diversity Mission Statement

Diversity is an opportunity

Morgan Stanley is only as effective as the people we employ. Our professionals have made our firm a preeminent provider of global financial services, with more than 600 offices in 28 countries. It is our 55,000 employees who are our key advantage in delivering world-class service to our clients and positive results to our shareholders. Therefore, our commitment to diversity in all aspects of our franchise begins with our most valuable resource-our people. To maintain our position of leadership, we continually seek the broadest knowledge possible of the global markets in which we operate. Our workforce must consist of the most talented and creative individuals who represent a cross-section of our global community. Different perspectives allow us to retain our competitive edge and to provide the best service possible to our clients in accordance with the Morgan Stanley hallmarks of quality, innovation and integrity.

At Morgan Stanley, we value and embrace differences. Our commitment to diversity permeates all levels of our organization. By fostering a corporate culture that is open and inclusive, our employees can achieve their individual professional goals and Morgan Stanley can achieve its vision: "Connecting people, ideas and capital, we will be the world's first choice for achieving financial aspirations."

Additional Information

Career development

For Morgan Stanley to remain a preeminent global financial services firm, continuous development of our people is critical. Our core values – integrity, excellence, entrepreneurial spirit, respect for individuals and cultures and teamwork-will continue to help us attract and develop the most diverse and exceptional individuals who will shape and strengthen our business culture. We focus on enhancing the careers of our employees by offering a variety of educational and professional development programs. In addition to our Minority Business Exchange, which is one of our minority focused development programs, Morgan Stanley also has numerous career development programs designed specifically for women. Our internal women's conferences focus on enhancing the professional skills of our female employees. Many of the senior women at Morgan Stanley are active participants in these conferences and share their best practices on developing skills ranging from business development to networking and mentoring to marketing to technical skills. Some of these events include our Women's Business Exchange, our Divisional Women's Leadership Conferences and our Leadership and Networking Initiative (LANI). Our efforts with respect to the advancement of women recently received national recognition by *Essence* magazine which selected Morgan Stanley as one of the "30 Best Companies for Black Women" and by *Working Mother* magazine which named the firm one of the "100 Best Companies for Working Mothers."

Work-life programs

Our commitment to diversity extends to the work-life initiatives that address the challenge of balancing home and career. These life-enhancing services are as broad-based and varied as the workforce they support. Our work-life programs include Child and Elder Care, Adoption Assistance and Flexible Work Arrangements. Our Wellness Program educates employees on the benefits of physical exercise, weight control and good nutrition. The Health Units and the Fitness Centers conduct CPR training, screenings for tuberculosis, glaucoma and prostate cancer, blood tests for diabetes, nutritional counseling, weight management seminars and various inoculations. In addition to our Employee Assistance Program, we offer on-site Lamaze classes, new parent kits, lactation rooms for nursing mothers, "quiet rooms" for employees and on-site seminars that cover a host of personal and work-related issues. Our College Coach program provides counseling to all employees and their children on the college application process, including financial aid. By offering options and services that are flexible, inclusive and leading-edge, we continually strive to enable our employees to navigate more easily the challenges of everyday life.

Supplier diversity

We take diversity seriously in all aspects of our business-including the companies that supply us with the wide array of products and services that enable us to serve our customers. Our program identifies women- and minority-owned companies that can offer cost-effective solutions to our business needs. Working with women- and minority-owned businesses not only fosters strategic and mutually advantageous business relationships, but has the added benefit of stimulating economic development and strengthening the communities in which we do business. We look to develop longstanding relationships with partners who are visionaries and whose creativity, ethical business practices and entrepreneurial spirit will keep Morgan Stanley at the forefront of the financial services industry.

Charitable contributions

Morgan Stanley has a proven track record of assisting charitable organizations that provide opportunities, access and information to those most in need. Through corporate contributions and support from our U.S. and international foundations, we contribute millions of dollars to charitable organizations, providing support to more than 900 cities across the globe.

In 2004, Morgan Stanley contributed over $33 million to charitable organizations and supported a broad range of programs in the arts, education, developmental youth programs, health and human services and community development. More than 2,400 charities, many of which specifically address issues particularly relevant to women and minorities, are the recipients of our support. In addition to firm funding, our 55,000 employees personally contribute more than $6 million towards charitable efforts on an annual basis.

Community outreach

Morgan Stanley encourages and supports employee volunteerism. Our employees are engaged in a wide variety of volunteer activities. Through our Volunteer Incentive Program (VIP), Morgan Stanley augments the time donated by our employees with grants to hundreds of health and social service organizations in which our employees are involved, many of which may not have access to traditional sources of funding.

Morgan Stanley has also implemented a Diversity Sponsorship Initiative, which sponsors programs that celebrate accomplishments, champion aspirations and promote awareness of women, minorities and other diverse groups while inspiring younger generations to view the world as boundless. As part of this initiative, Morgan Stanley signed on as the national sponsor for the Alvin Ailey American Dance Theater Tours 2004 and 2005, which enables Ailey to deliver school-based outreach initiatives in 10 cities across the country. The firm also commemorated the 50th anniversary of the Supreme Court's groundbreaking decision that ended legal segregation in the United States by being the Title Sponsor of Separate is Not Equal: Brown v. Board of Education, a year-long exhibit at the Smithsonian's National Museum of American History in Washington D.C. In conjunction with this exhibition, Morgan Stanley is also sponsoring a series of educational programs for middle and high school students.

2004 Awards

- The American Indian College Fund honored Morgan Stanley at its annual dinner for its commitment to and work with the College Fund

- *Black Collegian* magazine named Morgan Stanley as one of the "Top 50 Diversity Employers"

- *Working Mother* magazine named Morgan Stanley as one of the "100 Best Companies for Working Mothers"

- *Family Digest* magazine named Morgan Stanley as one of the "Best Companies for African-Americans"

- *Essence* magazine named Morgan Stanley as one of the "30 Best Companies for Black Women"

- *Asian Enterprise* magazine named Morgan Stanley as one of the "Top Companies for Asian-Americans"

- *Hispanic* magazine selected Morgan Stanley as one of the "100 Companies Providing the Most Opportunities to Hispanics"

Conclusion

We are deeply committed to maintaining a diverse workforce at Morgan Stanley and to providing a workplace that nurtures, challenges and inspires. Each and every individual in our franchise has his or her own distinct identity forged from a unique set of abilities, life experiences, interests, talents and background. Our environment, which welcomes differences, allows the unique resources of our people to help us achieve our firm's goals and aspirations. Through the success of our inclusive, collaborative efforts, we have a preeminent global financial services Firm – the "First Choice" for our employees, our clients and our shareholders. That is why at Morgan Stanley, diversity is not an obligation... it's an opportunity. An opportunity to meet challenges, to effect change and to achieve goals.

TD Securities

31 West 52nd Street
19th Floor
New York, NY 10019
Phone: (212) 827-7000
Fax: (212) 827-7248
www.tdsecurities.com

Locations

U.S. (New York, Baltimore, Chicago, Houston, Miami, San Diego)
Mexico City
Canada (Toronto, Montreal, Calgary, Vancouver)
U.K. (London, Dublin)
Asia (Hong Kong, Tokyo, Singapore, Taipei, Sydney, Mumbai, Seoul)

Contact Information

Recruiting Contact Person:
Kesi J. Green, HR Recruitment Specialist

Diversity URL:
www.td.com/hr/diversity.jsp

E-mail:
recruiter@tdsecurities.com

Strategic Plan and Diversity Leadership

How does the firm's leadership communicate the importance of diversity to everyone at the firm?
Through e-mails, web site, meetings and newsletters

Who has primary responsibility for leading overall diversity initiatives at your firm?
Diversity Leadership Council

Does your firm currently have a diversity committee? Yes

If yes, does the committee's representation include one or more members of the firm's management/executive committee (or the equivalent)? Yes

If yes, how many senior managers are on the committee, and how often did the committee convene in furtherance of the firm's diversity initiatives in 2004?

Total senior managers on committee: 11
Number of diversity meetings annually: 4-6

Does the committee(s) and/or diversity leader establish and set goals or objectives consistent with management's priorities? Yes

Has the firm undertaken a formal or informal diversity program or set of initiatives aimed at increasing the diversity of the firm? Yes

How often does the firm's management review the firm's diversity progress/results? Monthly

Are the members of the diversity committee or committees involved in diversity activities?
Working groups include: serving diverse and multicultural communities; expanding leadership opportunities for women; expanding leadership opportunities for visible minorities; enhancing recruitment and promotion for persons with disabilities; and enhancing and promoting an inclusive environment for gay and lesbian employees and customers.

Recruitment of New Analysts & Associates

On-campus

Please list the schools at which you recruit.

Ivy League schols: Columbia University, Cornell University

Public state schools: University of Illinois at Urbana-Champaign, University of Illinois at Chicago, Penn State University, Queen's University (Canada), University of Toronto (Canada), University of Waterloo (Canada), University of Western Ontario (Canada), Wilfred Laurier University (Canada)

Private schools: Emory University, DePaul University, Illinois Institute of Technology, Northwestern University, University of Chicago, Boston College, MIT, NYU, Georgetown University

Of the schools that you listed above, are there any special outreach efforts directed to encourage minority students to consider your firm?

- Advertise in minority student association publications
- Sponsor minority student association events
- Outreach to leadership of minority student organizations
- National Black MBA Association, Robert Toigo Foundation
- Professional Recruiting

What activities does the firm undertake to attract women and minorities?

- Partner programs with women and minority banking associations
- Seek referrals from other professionals
- Utilize online job services
- Catalyst, Women in Capital Markets Forum, Robert Toigo Foundation, National Black MBA Association

Internships

Summer Analyst & Associate Program

Deadline for application for the internship: mid-February
Number of interns in the program in summer 2005: 8
Length of the program (in weeks): 10
Program web site: www.tdsecurities.com/careers

Summer interns assume similar responsibilities to the full-time Analysts and Associates in that they are looked upon as vital resources, providing creative input in a variety of disciplines. Working with clients in a variety of industries, interns gain exposure to different business models and industry dynamics. The internship program provides students with a broad exposure to the firm and a more specific experience in a particular business. Each summer intern is assigned to a specific business group for most of the internship. We do everything to ensure that the intern has the opportunity to have a meaningful experience through either deal exposure or involvement in a project, or some combination thereof. To supplement their exposure to the broader scope of our operations, we conduct business presentations which are intended to cover the basics of each business and all TD products.

Entry-level Programs/Full-time Opportunities/Training Programs

Full-time Analyst & Associate Training Program

Length of program: 5 weeks
Geographic location(s) of program: New York & Toronto

Please describe the training/training component of this program: Financial Modeling, Accounting, Series 7 and Credit Analysis Training; Business Group Presentations; social events; Toronto Headquarters office visit (Teambuilding, Communication and Presentation Skills Training, Bloomberg Training)

Tuition reimbursement is available for all full-time employees. TD Securities encourages employees to continue to upgrade their knowledge and skills through the use of work-related, external educational courses and when personal costs are incurred, will provide financial support to the extent of this policy, when employees are successful in completing such courses.

Diversity Mission Statement

Diversity at TD Bank Financial Group (TD) is about providing a supportive environment that recognizes differences and allows everyone to achieve their potential. At TD, we believe that diversity is key to our success in the competitive global marketplace. By embracing people with a wide range of unique experiences and abilities, we embrace the world. We open the door to innovation and cultivate positive change. We make our business stronger.

We strive to build a culture of inclusion - one that respects and recognizes the individual skills and perspectives of every employee - and to create and succeed in a workplace where all employees have the opportunity to reach their full potential.

As part of our team, you will be treated fairly and recognized and rewarded for your ability. You'll have access to opportunity for career growth and promotion.

You'll work in a culture that actively supports respect and tolerance. Through our Respect in the Workplace Program, for instance, we strive to eliminate harassment by building a greater awareness of issues and, as importantly, having an established process to respond to complaints.

At TD, you'll benefit too from our strong commitment to employment equity. Employment equity means we break down the barriers to job opportunities whether they are accidental, unintentional or systemic.

Our policy is simple. We hire, train, develop, promote and compensate everyone on the basis of ability, potential and performance. We have a long-term commitment to the removal of discriminatory or arbitrary barriers. And we keep a constant eye on our workplace to ensure employment equity is upheld.

At TD, we want you to feel at home. We want you to excel, to connect with others at work, to grow and to discover.

Rewarding careers with global opportunities.
It starts with you.

UBS is one of the world's leading financial firms, employing over 68,000 people in 50 countries. Our wealth management, global asset management and investment banking businesses offer clients a wide range of products and services designed to help them meet their individual needs and goals.

We seek highly talented individuals who can bring something different to our organization and offer them superb career opportunities to match their potential.

Our people reflect a diversity of views and cultures that is unique in the industry. UBS is committed to an open and meritocratic environment where every employee has the opportunity to thrive and excel, supported by some of the best development and training programs in the industry.

It starts with you.

www.ubs.com/graduates

UBS is an equal opportunity employer committed to diversity in its workforce.

| Wealth Management | Global Asset Management | Investment Bank |

You & Us

UBS

© UBS 2005. All rights reserved.

UBS Investment Bank

1285 Avenue of the Americas
New York, NY 10019
(212) 821-3000
www.ubs.com/diversity

Locations

Locations in over 60 countries.

Contact Information

Contact Person: Donald Franklin, Diversity Recruiter
E-mail: diversityrecruiting@ubs.com

Strategic Plan and Diversity Leadership

How does the firm's leadership communicate the importance of diversity to everyone at the firm?
Our leaders are very committed to diversity and it is communicated in a number of ways: town halls, videos, brochures, e-mails, memo, intranet sites, diversity events and newsletters.

Who has primary responsibility for leading overall diversity initiatives at your firm?
Mona Lau, Global Head, Group Diversity

Who has primary responsibility for diversity recruiting initiatives at your firm, if different from (a)?
Donald Franklin, Diversity Recruiter

Does your firm currently have a diversity committee? Yes

If yes, does the committee's representation include one or more members of the firm's management/executive committee (or the equivalent)? Yes

If yes, how many senior managers are on the committee, and how often did the committee convene in furtherance of the firm's diversity initiatives in 2004?

Number of diversity meetings annually: Numerous

If you have more than one diversity committee, please list:
Diversity Advisory Council, Executive Diversity Council, Regional Diversity Boards, Minority Leadership Council. We have regional diversity boards in 10 locations globally comprised of Senior Managers across businesses in the U.S., UK, France, Germany, Italy, Spain, Switzerland, Asia, Japan, Australia. In addition we have a number of diversity committees at the business unit level.

Does the committee(s) and/or diversity leader establish and set goals or objectives consistent with management's priorities? Yes

Has the firm undertaken a formal or informal diversity program or set of initiatives aimed at increasing the diversity of the firm? Yes, formal

How often does the firm's management review the firm's diversity progress/results?

Senior Management reviews diversity progress on an ongoing basis.

How is the firm's diversity committee(s) and/or firm management held accountable for achieving results?
Diversity is one of the ten core values at UBS. Execution of the diversity strategy is an integral part of the performance review process.

Are the members of the diversity committee or committees involved in diversity activities? Yes. Recruiting, mentoring programs, training programs, community service.

- **Global:** Career development programs for women and minorities; hosted global professional recruiting breakfast series to educate and encourage search firm partners to diversify candidate slates; multiple employee networks globally

- **Australia:** UBS Young Women Leadership Academy for 25 public high school students

- **U.S.:** Mentoring Up program; Women's Career Development Pilot Workshop for All Bar None Steering Committee; Annual UBS Diversity Celebration

- **China:** UBS Women in Financial Services Conference for 75 female executives and clients

- **Germany:** Segment marketing activities to build female, Latin American and mature client bases; Women's Business Network conference

- **APAC:** Women's Development Alliance (WDA) program for high potential women in Japan

- **Switzerland:** Cross-cultural workshop on how to effectively manage global teams; workshop on how to attract women branch managers

- **UK:** Interbank Campus Recruiting events for undergraduate female, LGBT and minority students

Recruitment of New Analysts & Associates

On-campus

Please list the schools at which your firm recruits.

- Ivy League schools
- Public state schools
- Private schools

- Historically Black Colleges and Universities (HBCUs)
- Hispanic Serving Institutions (HSIs)
- Other predominantly minority and/or women's colleges

Do you have any special outreach efforts directed to encourage minority students to consider your firm?

- Hold a reception for minority students
- Conferences: NSHMBA, MBMBAA, SHPE, NSBE, NHBA, Thurgood Marshall
- Advertise in minority student association publication(s)
- Participate in/host minority student job fair(s)
- Sponsor minority student association events
- Firm's professionals participate on career panels at school
- Outreach to leadership of minority student organizations
- Scholarships or intern/fellowships for minority students

Professional Recruiting

What activities does the firm undertake to attract women and minorities?

- *Partner programs with women and minority banking associations:* Financial Women's Association, Women's Bond Club
- *Conferences:* Linkage – Diversity Conference, NSHMBA, NBMBAA, SHPE, NSBE
- *Participate at minority job fairs:* To name a few: Women for Hire, Career Fair for Women and Minorities, NY Times Job Market Diversity Career Fair, Urban Financial Services Coalition
- Seek referrals from other professionals
- *Utilize online job services:* Monster.com, careerbuilder.com

Do you use executive recruiting/search firms to seek to identify new diversity hires? Yes

Internships

Name of internship program: Investment Banking, Sales & Trading, Operations, Information Technology, Financial Control, Equity Research, COO Internship Program, SEO Program, AlumniAthlete Network Program
Deadline for application for the internship: Spring semester
Length of the program: 10 weeks

Web site for internship information: www.ubs.com/graduates

Scholarships

Name of scholarship program: Diversity Scholarship
Deadline for application for the scholarship program: Late fall
Web site or other contact information for scholarship:
diversityrecruiting@ubs.com

Affinity Groups/Employee Networks

All Bar None

The mission of the network is to promote the recruitment, retention and advancement of women at UBS. It also provides networking, mentoring and leadership opportunities that encourage the professional and personal development of all employees.

The Cultural Awareness Network

This network raises awareness of the broad diversity of cultures within UBS and our business presence around the world, fosters an environment that leverages the culture of our members, and provides a forum to promote cross-cultural understanding among all employees.

League of Employees of African Descent

A forum to strengthen diversity within UBS, by helping members grow professionally through: training and development, career management and networking opportunities. This employee group ultimately strives to promote the recruitment, advancement and retention of employees of African descent within UBS in the Americas.

UBS Pride

LGBT Network. It maximizes all employees' contributions by creating and sustaining a LGBT friendly environment where people are comfortable being open and honest about their individuality.

Entry-level Programs/Full-time Opportunities

Name of program: Investment Bank Opportunities: Graduate Development Program (Information Technology), Analyst Training Program (Investment Banking Department), Graduate Training Program (Equities and Fixed Income), Associate Training Program (Operations)
Length of program: 12-18 months
Geographic location(s) of program: Global

Please describe the training/training component of this program.

- 6- to 8-week training program that covers the building of technical skills, knowledge of UBS, and a support network

- Educational courses focusing on personal and professional effectiveness skills - presentation, influencing, time management skills, etc.

- Social and networking opportunities with fellow graduates and senior management

- Ongoing performance reviews and objective setting

Diversity Mission Statement

UBS will only achieve its global business objectives if we respect and promote differences in background, perspectives and expertise. This in turn will promote creativity and innovation and create business opportunities. Creating a culture of diversity and inclusion is critical to the success of our global business.

Additional Information

At UBS, we promote a work environment that encourages all our talented employees to excel and advance. Employee networks and councils, talent development programs, and a broad range of work life balance options all play a part in creating an inclusive and friendly atmosphere.

The Minority Leadership Council (MLC) is a cross-business group of Hispanic and African American Managing Directors, Executive Directors and Senior Vice Presidents who meet periodically to ensure that UBS continues to create a welcoming work environment for minority talent. Along with the MLC, UBS and its senior leaders take great pride in the strength and global reach of UBS's employee networks. Recruitment, retention, advancement and promotion of an inclusive environment are the key deliverables of the League of Employees of African Descent (LEAD), Cultural Awareness Networks (CAN), 13 global women's networks including All Bar None in the UK and US, the Women's Business Network (WBN) which operates in Germany and Switzerland, and networks formed for the gay and lesbian employee population, such as UBS Pride.

UBS has mandatory training for senior management focusing on managing in a diverse environment. UBS also presents workshops tailored to women and minorities that focus on cultivating skills and strategies for success. The workshops provide an opportunity to learn and share tips for responding to the challenges inherent to the financial industry's fast-paced, demanding environment.

The challenge of running a global firm and supporting work life balance offers UBS the opportunity to actively promote flexible work arrangements where feasible, including telecommuting and job shares. Childcare options are also available in many locations. This has been recognized by *Working Mothers* (100 Best Companies) and the Human Rights Campaign (Score of 100).

Partnerships with organizations and foundations demonstrate UBS's continuing commitment to attracting a diverse pool of talented future employees. UBS is proud to support the 100 Black Men, AlumniAthlete Network, A Better Chance, Capital Chance, "I Have A Dream" Foundation, Executive Leadership Council, The Hispanic Scholarship Fund, INROADS, Management Leadership for Tomorrow, National Black MBA Association, National Society of Hispanics MBAs, Sponsors for Educational Opportunity, the Windsor Fellowship and many others

As a global firm, community affairs must exemplify its broad approach; UBS has met the challenge through outreach programs around the world including Africa, the Americas, Asia-Pacific and Europe. UBS' key partnerships in the Americas region include After School Matters, the Children's Aid Society, the Coalition for the Homeless, and the Committee for Democracy in Information Technology, the Juvenile Diabetes Research Foundation and the Stamford Public Schools.

WHAT CAN AN
ART FORM
TEACH US ABOUT
DIVERSITY IN THE WORKPLACE?

■

Its foundation is built on talent, originality and a desire for expression

Extraordinary performances create an indelible impact. When it comes to your career, think about the impact an environment will have on your ability to achieve. Will it inspire? Will it be rich with culture and people who are interested in what you have to contribute? At Wachovia, we recognize the value of individuals with differing backgrounds and experiences as a cornerstone of our success. We demonstrate, each day, that the concept of mutual respect and integrity means much more to us than just words. For more information on opportunities with Wachovia, please visit us online at **wachovia.com/college**.

WACHOVIA

Uncommon Wisdom

©2004 Wachovia Corporation　　　　　　　　　　　　　　　　　　Wachovia recognizes and values diversity. EOE, M/F/D/V.

Wachovia

301 S. College St.
Suite 4000
One Wachovia Center
Charlotte, NC 28288-0013
Phone: 704-374-6161
www.wachovia.com

Locations

Full financial services through offices in 15 states:
Connecticut • New York • New Jersey • Pennsylvania • Delaware • Maryland • Virginia • North Carolina • South Carolina • Georgia • Florida • Alabama • Tennessee • Mississippi • Texas • Washington, D.C.

Full-service retail brokerage with offices in 49 states through Wachovia Securities, LLC. Global services through 33 international offices.

The Stats

Assets: $507 billion (average)
Deposits: $295 billion
Stockholders' Equity: $46 billion

Strategic Plan and Diversity Leadership

How does the firm's leadership communicate the importance of diversity to everyone at the firm?
Meeting diversity goals is tied to compensation. We have an Office of Diversity as well as of Diversity Recruiting.

Who has primary responsibility for leading overall diversity initiatives at your firm?

Edna Norwood
Director of Diversity

Does your firm currently have a diversity committee? Yes

If yes, does the committee's representation include one or more members of the firm's management/executive committee (or the equivalent)? Yes

If yes, how many senior managers are on the committee, and how often did the committee convene in furtherance of the firm's diversity initiatives in 2004?
The committee meets quarterly. It includes all operation committee members and some other senior managers.

Number of diversity meetings annually: 4

If you have more than one diversity committee, please list.
We have one committee at the corporate level and several others in specific business units.

Does the committee(s) and/or diversity leader establish and set goals or objectives consistent with management's priorities? Yes

Has the firm undertaken a formal or informal diversity program or set of initiatives aimed at increasing the diversity of the firm? Yes, formal

How often does the firm's management review the firm's diversity progress/results? Quarterly

How is the firm's diversity committee(s) and/or firm management held accountable for achieving results?
Through compensation and operational goals

Are the members of the diversity committee or committees involved in diversity activities? Yes, numerous diversity activities

Recruitment of New Analysts & Associates

On-campus

Please list the schools at which your firm recruits.

- Ivy League schools
- Public state schools
- Private schools
- Historically Black Colleges and Universities (HBCUs)
- Hispanic Serving Institutions (HSIs)

Of the schools that you listed above, do you have any special outreach efforts directed to encourage minority students to consider your firm?

- Hold a reception for minority students
- Conferences: INROADS, TOIGO, NBMBA/NHMBA, other school events
- Advertise in minority student association publications
- Participate in/host minority student job fairs
- Sponsor minority student association events
- Firm's professionals participate on career panels at school
- Outreach to leadership of minority student organizations
- Scholarships or intern/fellowships for minority students

What activities does the firm undertake to attract women and minorities?

- Partner programs with women and minority banking associations
- Conferences
- Participate at minority job fairs
- Seek referrals from other professionals
- Utilize online job services

Do you use executive recruiting/search firms to seek to identify new diversity hires? Yes

Internships

> *Deadline for application for the internship:* The majority are recruited spring semester
> *Number of interns in the program in summer 2004:* 150
> *Pay:* Varies
> *Length of the program:* 10 – 12 weeks

Percentage of interns in the program who receive offers of full-time employment: 60%

Please see our web site for more internship information: www.Wachovia.com/college

Please also see our web site for more information on scholarships, entry-level opportunities, training programs and affinity groups.

Diversity Mission Statement

Wachovia's Diversity Values Statement

Diversity at Wachovia is a business imperative. Aligning with our customer base, engaging our communities, and attracting and retaining talented individuals are critical to our success. We are committed to long-term positive culture change and seek to incorporate diversity into all aspects of our business. Every individual at Wachovia has an ongoing responsibility to advance diversity.

We are committed to being an inclusive company where all people are treated fairly, recognized for their individuality, promoted based on performance, and encouraged to reach their full potential. We believe in recognizing, understanding, and respecting differences among all people. These differences include but are not limited to race, gender, sexual orientation, work/life status, ethnic origin, culture, spiritual beliefs and practices, age, level, physical/mental ability and veteran status.

"In order for Wachovia to reach its true potential, we must continue to build an organization that values individual differences. Our focus is on creating an inclusive workplace..."

Ken Thompson, CEO

William Blair & Company

222 W. Adams Street
Chicago, IL 60606
Phone (312) 236-1600
www.williamblair.com

Locations

Chicago, IL (HQ)
Hartford, CT
San Francisco, CA

London
Tokyo
Vaduz
Zurich

Diversity at William Blair & Company

Recruitment is one of the first steps in creating a more diverse environment. William Blair & Company, L.L.C.'s recruiting philosophy is to attract and retain the most talented and qualified individuals to the firm regardless of race, gender, religion, etc. To that end, when we publicly post a job, we put it on William Blair & Company's web site, as well as on Career Builder. Career Builder is affiliated with the Chicago Tribune and is the preferred job board for targeting local candidates. Furthermore, Career Builder has hundreds of partnerships with other career sites that target diverse candidates, such as Womens Wall Street, Women in Business & Industry, U.S. Diversity and Hispanic Today. A posting on Career Builder will be seen by diverse candidates who visit the career pages of those web sites.

William Blair & Company's investment banking group posts its analyst program positions at diverse schools, including Spelman College, Howard University and Morehouse College. The analyst class starting the summer of 2005 will comprise more than 70% women (although not due to any strategic change in the way recruiting is done).

William Blair & Company was highlighted in *Chicago* magazine as one of the "25 Best Places to Work." The firm is ranked #18 and earned the seventh-highest employee score. The article, which ran in the October 2004 issue, emphasizes the firm's employee ownership, collegial atmosphere, and flexible work schedule.

William Blair & Company supports professional business efforts:
Chicago Summer Business Institute – William Blair & Company annually finances business internships for inner-city high school students, sponsored by the city of Chicago.

Cristo Rey Jesuit High School Internship Program – William Blair & Company provides students of this primarily Hispanic high school the opportunity to have "real" job experiences and allows them to earn a large portion of their tuition costs. The students fill entry-level positions within the firm on a part-time basis and are compensated on an hourly basis.

Neighborhood Rejuvenation Partners – William Blair & Company acted as an agent to raise nearly $20 million for Neighborhood Rejuvenation Partners, for the redevelopment of the South Side after the project buildings are razed.

William Blair & Company Scholarship Program – For the past few years, the company has provided scholarships for two children each year from the Brown Elementary School, located on Chicago's West Side. Portfolio managers invest the money and provide financial counseling through the high school years to encourage these children to graduate and use the funds for college.

EMPLOYER DIRECTORY

ABN AMRO Holding N.V.

Gustav Mahlerlaan 10
1082 PP
Amsterdam, The Netherlands
Phone: +31-20-628-9393
www.abnamro.com

Locations

3,446 offices in more than 60 countries

The Stats

Total Employees: 97,276
Revenue (2004): $45,139 million

Employment Contact

www.abnamro.com/com/career/home.jsp

This information is taken from publicly available sources.

Employment Opportunities

We welcome newcomers who share our ambitions. At ABN AMRO, fulfilling ambitions – both yours and ours – goes hand in hand with a human and supportive way of working. Yes, we believe in creating maximum economic value for our clients and shareholders, but not at the expense of human values and principles.

Diversity Information

ABN AMRO is an equal opportunities employer.

ABN AMRO is committed to providing equal opportunities in employment. We will not discriminate between applications for reasons of gender, race, religion, colour, nationality, ethnic origin, sexual orientation, marital status, age or disability.

ABN AMRO employs over 110,000 full-time equivalent staff members in more than 60 countries and is committed to embracing diversity. At ABN AMRO diversity is about each individual coming to terms with his or her attitudes, beliefs and expectations about others and gaining comfort with difference.

We are on a journey to become a truly inclusive and equitable organisation – one that makes full use of the contributions of all employees. In addition to being a moral and social responsibility, we believe this is also steeped in good business sense. An environment where all employees feel included and valued yields greater commitment and motivation. We not only benefit from the creativity that diverse perspectives can inspire, we also enjoy the greater productivity and competitive advantage that comes from being an attractive employer for talented employees from all walks of life.

Web address for diversity: www.abnamro.com/com/career/jobs_map_alt.jsp

This information is taken from publicly available sources.

Allen & Company

711 Fifth Avenue, 9th Floor
New York, NY 10022
Phone: (212) 832-8000

Locations

New York, NY

The Stats

Total Employees: 200

This information is taken from publicly available sources.

The Blackstone Group

345 Park Avenue
New York, NY 10154
Phone: (212) 583-5000
Fax: (212) 583-5712
www.blackstone.com

Locations

New York, NY (HQ)
Atlanta, GA
Boston, MA
Hamburg
London

Employment Contact

www.blackstone.com/careers/index.html
E-mail: analyst_recruiting@
  blackstone.com
summeranalyst_recruiting@
  blackstone.com
associate_recruiting@blackstone.com
summer_associate_recruiting@
  blackstone.com

This information is taken from publicly available sources.

Employment Opportunities

Full time program

Blackstone's full-time analyst recruiting process begins in the fall with a variety of informational events at target schools, including firm presentations, receptions and/or dinners with our recruiting team. Such events are followed by formal interviews, either on or off-campus, depending upon the school. If Blackstone does not conduct on-campus interviews at your school, please submit your resume on the Blackstone web site.

After first round interviews are concluded, selected students are invited to the New York office for a multi-round process during which they will meet one-on-one with various members within the group to which they are applying.

Candidates who receive an offer will begin their employment in early July with an intensive three-week training program covering the basics of accounting, corporate finance, financial modeling, an overview of corporate history and operations, as well as a review of Blackstone's technology systems and database capabilities.

The recommended timing to apply for a full-time analyst position is early September of senior year. Please submit a cover letter and resume to the recruiting department via e-mail at analyst_recruiting@blackstone.com.

Internship program

The summer analyst recruiting process begins in January at target schools, including receptions and/or dinners with the recruiting team. Such events are followed by formal interviews, both on and off-campus. Blackstone representatives cannot visit every school. If Blackstone do not conduct on-campus interviews at your school, please submit your resume via the link below and the company will contact you directly.

After first round interviews are concluded, selected students are invited to the New York office for a multi-round process during which you will meet one-on-one with various members of the group to which you are applying.

Candidates who receive an offer will begin their summer employment in early June. The Internship Program is approximately 10 weeks in length.

The recommended timing to apply for a summer analyst position is late December of your junior year. summer analyst Internships are for rising seniors only. Please submit a cover letter and resume to our recruiting department via e-mail at summer_analyst_recruiting@blackstone.com, or fax at (212) 583 5167.

This information is taken from publicly available sources.

BNP Paribas Group

787 Seventh Avenue
The Equitable Tower
New York, NY 10019
Phone: (212) 841-2000
Fax: (212) 841-2146
www.bnpparibas.com

Locations

2,200 in more than 85 countries worldwide

The Stats

Total Employees (2004): 94,900

Employment Contact

www.careers.bnpparibas.com/
E-mail: recruiting@americas.bnpparibas.com

This information is taken from publicly available sources.

Internship Opportunies

Internship positions offered to graduates provide an excellent opportunity to participate in the developments and innovations taking place in the field of banking. Positions are available across a wide range of activities, from Retail Banking to Corporate Finance, including Market Finance and Transversal Functions (Marketing, Information Systems, Auditing and Management Control).

The Group has solid roots in Europe, leading positions in Asia and an active presence in the United States. As such, applicants are invited to submit an application to the HR Department of their chosen location.

This information is taken from publicly available sources.

Calyon Securities (USA) Inc.

1301 Avenue of the Americas
New York, NY 10019
Phone: (212) 261-7000
Fax: (212) 459-3170
www.clamericas.com

Locations

15 offices in the U.S., France, Central and South America

Employment Contact

E-mail: hr@us.calyon.com

This information is taken from publicly available sources.

Employment Opportunities

Technology Co-op Program

Calyon in the Americas participates in Cooperative Education Programs with Stevens Institute of Technology and New Jersey Institute of Technology, giving university students an opportunity to get professional work experience while still in school. It allows students to combine classroom study with periods of paid professional employment which are directly related to their university major and career goals.

Building on its selection as a top 10 co-op employer (as recognized by the New Jersey Institute of Technology in 2000), Credit Lyonnais (now called Calyon) continues to contribute to the education, training and employment of students. Web site address for employment: www.clamericas.com/content/career_opportunities.asp

This information is taken from publicly available sources.

Cascadia Capital

403 Columbia Street,
Suite 500
Seattle, WA 98104
Phone: (206) 357-9100
Fax: (206).357-9101
www.cascadiacapital.com

Locations

New York, NY
Seattle, WA

Employment Contact

E-mail: hr@cascadiacapital.com.

This information is taken from publicly available sources.

Employment Opportunities

Cascadia Capital is made up of bright, committed and accomplished professionals. If you are interested in career opportunities with Cascadia Capital, e-mail your resume to hr@cascadiacapital.com.

Cascadia Capital is an Equal Opportunity Employer. Web site address for employment: www.cascadiacapital.com/careers.php

This information is taken from publicly available sources.

Chanin Capital Partners

11150 Santa Monica Blvd.
6th Floor
Los Angeles, CA 90025
Phone: (310) 445-4010
Fax: (310) 445-4028
www.chanin.com

Locations

Los Angeles, CA (HQ)
New York, NY
London

This information is taken from publicly available sources.

Employment Opportunities

Chanin Capital Partners hires interns and recent college graduates based on its business needs. Submit your resume and cover letter to the Los Angeles office and indicate the positions and offices for which you'd like to be considered. Web site address for employment: www.chanin.com/index.php3?id=700

E-mail: jshorr@chanin.com

Chanin Capital Partners is an Equal Opportunity Employer.

Dresdner Kleinwort Wasserstein

1301 Avenue of the Americas, New York, NY 10019
Phone: (212) 969-2700
www.drkw.com

Locations

39 major locations in
Europe
North America
South America
Africa
Asia Pacific

Employment Contact

www.drkw.com/eng/careers/index.php

This information is taken from publicly available sources.

Employment Opportunities

DrKW is the investment bank of Dresdner Bank AG and a member of the Allianz Group. Headquartered in London and Frankfurt and with an international network of offices, DrKW provides a full range of investment banking products and services to European and international clients through its Capital Markets and Corporate Finance & Origination business lines.

DrKW offers opportunities across the business for exceptional graduates We are recruiting within Corporate Finance and Origination, Capital Markets (Sales, Trading, Research), IT and Global Risk Management.

The closing date for applications in New York is November 30th. Please email any questions to recruit-m&a@drkw.com or by regular mail to:

Frances A. Lyman, Director, Recruiting.
Dresdner Kleinwort Wasserstein,
1301 Avenue of the Americas
New York,
New York 10019

This information is taken from publicly available sources.

First Albany Companies

677 Broadway
Albany, NY 12207-2990
Phone: 518-447-8500
Fax: 518.447.8115
www.fac.com

Locations

Albany, NY (HQ)
Atlanta, GA
Boston, MA
Chadds Ford, PA
Chicago, IL
Dallas, TX
Hartford, CT
Houston, TX
Los Angeles, CA
Minneapolis, MN
Naples, FL
New York, NY
Oakbrook Terrace, IL
Pittsburgh, PA
Richmond, VA
Wellesley, MA

The Stats

Total Employees (2004): 448
Revenue (2004): $181.8 million

Employment Contact

www.fac.com/itemDetail.asp?
 categoryID=243&itemID=16358
E-mail: careers@fac.com

This information is taken from publicly available sources.

Friedman Billings Ramsey

1001 Nineteenth Street North
Arlington, VA 22209
Phone: 703.312.9500
Fax: 703.312.9501
www.fbr.com

Locations:

Arlington, VA (HQ)
Bethesda, MD
Boston, MA
Cleveland, OH
Dallas, TX
Denver, CO
Houston, TX
Irvine, CA
New York, NY
Portland, OR
San Francisco, CA
Seattle, WA
London
Vienna

The Stats

Total Employees (2004): 698
Revenue (2004): $1.05 billion

This information is taken from publicly available sources.

Employment Opportunities

FBR seeks diverse, qualified individuals who are creative and highly motivated. Its management structure fosters open communication and the flow of ideas throughout all levels of the organization. Employees enjoy business casual dress in an atmosphere that is highly professional, fast paced and innovative while offering significant growth opportunities. FBR encourages employees to advance their skills and knowledge through a tuition reimbursement program and support of employee training and development. FBR is situated in the Washington, D.C. metropolitan area.

Internships

The FBR internship program provides students with the opportunity to gain valuable experience in the securities industry while introducing top talent to FBR. The firm believes a strong internship program is the best way to recruit future FBR leaders.

The program is designed to allow students to enhance their academic backgrounds by providing challenging work assignments in a fast-paced environment. Internships are typically available in the following areas:

- Institutional Sales
- Equity Research
- Investment Banking
- Asset Management
- Accounting/Finance
- Enterprise Operations
- Corporate Communications
- Human Resources
- Information Technology
- Legal/Compliance

The program lasts for 10-12 weeks, beginning in late May/early June and ending mid-to-late August. In addition to job-specific experience, the program also includes Information Sessions that provide a forum to gain further understanding of investment banking, institutional brokerage, and the financial services industry; as well as team-building Intern Activities.

FBR is looking for highly motivated students who are interested in exploring future career paths in a realistic work environment. Interested graduate and undergraduate students who are majoring in finance, accounting, and business administration are encouraged to apply.

The web site address for employment is:
www.fbrcorp.com/company/careers/default.asp

This information is taken from publicly available sources.

Gleacher Partners

660 Madison Avenue
New York, NY 10021
Phone: (212) 418-4200
Fax: (212) 752-2711
www.gleacher.com

Locations

New York, NY (HQ)
London

The Stats

Total Employees: 50+

This information is taken from publicly available sources.

Employment Opportunities

Gleacher recruits on a limited basis and looks for a highly select group of individuals with outstanding analytical abilities, strong communication and interpersonal skills, high personal integrity and an ability to thrive in a fast-paced and entrepreneurial work environment.

Employment contact

Gleacher Partners LLC
660 Madison Avenue
19th Floor
New York, NY 10021
Attn: Analyst Recruiting
Tel: (212) 418-4200
Fax: (212) 846-4910
analyst.recruiting@gleacher.com

Web site address for employment: www.gleacher.com/contact/index.html

This information is taken from publicly available sources.

Greenhill & Co.

300 Park Avenue
New York, NY 10022
Phone: (212) 389-1500
www.greenhill-co.com

Locations

New York, NY (HQ)
Frankfurt
London

The Stats

Total Employees (2004): 127
Revenue (2004): $151.9 million

This information is taken from publicly available sources.

Employment Opportunities

Greenhill's New York office offers both full-time and summer analyst opportunities. The New York Analyst program is two years long and strong performers are offered the opportunity to remain with the firm as a third year analyst. Exceptional performers may be offered a direct promotion to associate after three years as an analyst.

For full-time analyst positions, the firm conducts interviews on campus at a limited number of universities during October and November of each year. If Greenhill does not recruit at your school, please submit a cover letter and resume to nyanalystrecruit@greenhill-co.com and the firm will contact you if interested.

The New York office also offers summer analyst opportunities for undergraduates in the summer before their senior year. Interviews for summer analyst positions typically occur in February and March. Applicants should submit a cover letter and resume to nyanalystrecruit@greenhill-co.com. We will contact you if interested. Web site address for employment: www.greenhill-co.com/careers/

This information is taken from publicly available sources.

Houlihan Lokey Howard & Zukin

1930 Century Park West
Los Angeles, CA 90067
Phone: (310) 553-8871
Fax: (216) 689-7009
www.hlhz.com

Locations

Atlanta
Chicago
Dallas
Los Angeles
Minneapolis
New York
San Francisco
Washington, D.C.
London

The Stats

Total Employees (2004): 900+

This information is taken from publicly available sources.

Employment Opportunities

An investment banking career at Houlihan Lokey focuses on providing professionals with opportunities for long-term growth in a dynamic environment. In such a setting, we offer a strong combination of transaction expertise, strategic thinking and market know-how that stimulate our financial staff to take initiative at each level of personal and professional development. In turn, we are able to achieve our primary objective: to structure and implement innovative solutions for clients that deliver results.

In particular, Houlihan Lokey's middle-market focus combined with record levels of engagements offer a unique opportunity for junior-level bankers seeking to build a solid foundation in investment banking. For recent graduates, the ability to work on middle-market transactions affords several key advantages typically unavailable at the "bulge-bracket" level, specifically:

- Enhanced exposure to an array of investment banking services across a variety of industries
- Increased client contact
- Greater responsibilities on deal teams

In accordance with the opportunities available to Houlihan Lokey employees, we seek a corresponding level of excellence that is only achieved by recruiting high-caliber candidates. We encourage you to learn more about career opportunities at Houlihan Lokey by choosing any of the options on the menu bar, and contacting us by mail, fax or through our on-line application. We also invite you to register your e-mail address with us so that we can inform you of Houlihan Lokey career recruiting events in your area.

Web site address for employment: careers.hlhz.com/

This information is taken from publicly available sources.

HSBC Bank USA

452 5th Avenue
New York, NY 10018
www.us.hsbc.com

Locations

New York, NY (HQ)
Approximately 420 offices in the U.S.

The Stats

Revenue (2004): $5,397 million

Employment Contact

www.hsbcusa.com/careers/careerdev.html

This information is taken from publicly available sources.

Diversity Information

HSBC fosters an environment where individual differences are appreciated and utilized to the advantage of our customers, employees, business partners and communities.

Employer of Choice Awards

Through its subsidiaries, HSBC has earned recognition as an "Employer of Choice" by numerous national and local publications including:

Black Data Processing Association and *WorkplaceDiversity.com*, "Best Companies for Blacks in Technology"
Business and Professional Women, "Employer of the Year," Sioux Falls, South Dakota
Computerworld, "100 Best Places to Work in IT"
Diversityinc.com, "Top 50 Companies for Diversity"
Fortune, "2003 Global Most Admired Companies"
G.I. Jobs, "Top 25 Most Military-Friendly Employers"
Inside Business, "Top 25 Best Places to Work in Hampton Roads, Virginia"
Jacksonville, "Top 25 Family-Friendly Companies"
Oregon Business, "Oregon's Best Companies to Work For"
Training, "Training Top 100"
Working Mother, "100 Best Companies for Working Mothers"

Diversity Recruiting

HSBC has partnered with minority professional organizations.

- INROADS, Inc.
- National Association of Asian American Professionals
- National Black MBA Association
- National Society of Hispanic MBAs
- National Association for the Advancement of Colored People
- National Urban League
- United Negro College Fund

Employee Network Groups

The following employee networking groups are currently offered at HSBC:

- African American
- Asian/Pacific Islander
- GLBT (gay/lesbian/bisexual/transgender employees)
- Hispanic/Latin American
- Indian Employee Network Group
- Native American
- People with Disabilities
- Women's Forum

Web site address for diversity: www.hsbcusa.com/diversity/workplace.html

This information is taken from publicly available sources.

Jefferies & Co.

520 Madison Avenue
New York, NY 10022
Phone: (212) 284-2550

Locations

New York, NY (HQ)
Atlanta, GA
Boston, MA
Chicago, IL
Dallas, TX
Denver, CO
Houston, TX
Jersey City, NJ
Los Angeles, CA
Nashville, TN
New Orleans, LA
Richmond, VA
San Francisco, CA
Short Hills, NJ
Silicon Valley, CA
Stamford, CT

London
Melbourne
Paris
Sydney
Tokyo
Zurich

The Stats

Total Employees (2004): 1783
Revenue (2004): $1198.6 million

Employment Contact

eastcoastrecruiting@jefferies.com

This information is taken from publicly available sources.

Keefe, Bruyette & Woods

The Equitable Building
787 Seventh Avenue,
4th Floor
New York, NY 10019
Phone: (212) 887-7777

Locations

New York, NY (HQ)
Atlanta, GA
Boston, MA
Chicago, IL
Columbus, OH
Hartford, CT
Hoboken, NJ
Richmond, VA
San Francisco, CA

Employment Contact

E-mail: recruiting@kbw.com

This information is taken from publicly available sources.

KeyCorp

127 Public Square
Cleveland, OH 44114
Phone: (216) 689-6300
Fax: (216) 689-7009
www.key.com

Locations

950 locations in 12 states

The Stats

Employees (2004): 19,576
Revenue (2004): $5,564 million

Employment Contact

www.keybank.com/html/A-3.html

This information is taken from publicly available sources.

Employment Opportunities

Undergraduate Programs

Key Undergraduate Programs help connect recent college graduates with exciting opportunities at Key. By combining on-the-job training, hands-on experience and department rotations, Key Analyst Program graduates are well prepared for a career with the firm.

Internships

Key internship programs offer college students an opportunity to experience working at Key on a short-term basis. Internships prepare students for full-time opportunities in the Undergraduate Programs and other opportunities upon graduation. Key recruits for its internship program at college campuses across the country and target undergraduate students who major in finance, business, accounting and information technology.

Internships also help to build a foundation of diversity at Key, as Key partners with organizations such as INROADS and the United Negro College Fund (UNCF).

Diversity Information

Diversity Awareness

We celebrate diversity at Key in many ways. We offer training, mentoring programs and partnerships to our employees and to our communities. Our goal is for employees to embrace diversity and value the differences that make each of us unique.

Training

Diversity Training – Valuing Differences – reinforces basic diversity concepts and provides skill-building exercises; training focuses on understanding oneself and others, cultural conflicts, resolving diversity conflicts, workplace behavior, managing diverse relationships and dealing with inappropriate humor in the workplace

Weatherhead Executive Experience (1Key Diversity Leadership Challenge) – provides diversity training for senior-level executives as part of the Weatherhead Executive Experience

Diversity Thought Leadership Series – offers senior executives and managers forums where renowned corporate leaders and human relations experts present issues about cultivating an inclusive work environment and its impact on economic growth

Mentoring

Mentoring helps employees confront barriers, providing exposure to critical decision-making and helps build relationships in informal and formal organizational networks – here, minority and female employees receive professional development coaching from executives

Employee Leadership

Diversity Councils – councils comprised of employees who represent a cross-section of the organization, help drive our diversity efforts with the full support of senior management

Board of Inclusion – comprised of senior level managers who represent various lines of businesses and strengthen our efforts to attract and retain a diverse workforce – we recognize the need for a diverse set of talents to be a leader in today's marketplace

Partnerships

Key partnerships include:

National Black MBA: The National Black MBA Association, Inc. (NBMBAA) is a non-profit organization of minority MBAs, business professionals, entrepreneurs and MBA students

National Society for Hispanic MBAs: National Society of Hispanic MBAs (NSHMBA) is a non-profit organization whose mission is fostering Hispanic leadership through graduate management, education and professional development to improve society

INROADS Program: An international, world-class non-profit organization that helps to recruit, source and develop talented young people of color

Esperanza: Serves the educational needs of Cleveland's Hispanic community since 1983 and offers programs for elementary, middle school and high school students

United Negro College Fund (UNCF): The oldest and most distinguished higher education assistance organization in the United States

Historically Black Colleges and Universities (HBCU): We have partnerships with the following nationally ranked HBCU colleges and universities: Hampton University, Morehouse College and Spelman College

Diversity Hiring Coalition: An active member of the Diversity Hiring Coalition in Maine where resources are shared to help Maine employers to increase, support and retain racial and ethnic diversity in the workplace

This information is taken from publicly available sources.

Lazard Ltd

30 Rockefeller Plaza
New York, NY 10020
Phone: (212) 632-6000
www.lazard.com

Locations

28 offices in the U.S., Europe and Asia

The Stats

**Total Employees
(as of March 31, 2005):** 2,343
Total Revenue (2004): $1.03 billion

Employment Contact

www.lazard.com/Careers/FA-NA-UG.html

This information is taken from publicly available sources.

Employment Opportunities

Each year, Lazard visits leading universities and business schools throughout the U.S. and Europe.

Analysts

Individuals typically join our Analyst Training Program directly from college. The program is two years in length, with potential promotion to third year analyst offered to exceptional performers.

Analysts begin by participating in an intensive six-week training course taught by outside professors and Lazard bankers. Analysts then become integral members of the Financial Advisory practice, joining small transaction teams which provide financial advisory services to the firm's clients. Assignments fall into a range of categories, including mergers and acquisitions, divestitures, general and strategic advisory services, corporate restructurings and capital markets.

Due to our small size and significant transaction volume, Lazard's analysts are expected to assume unusually significant levels of responsibility requiring a high degree of maturity, self-confidence and technical aptitude. Day-to-day responsibilities of an analyst include: financial analysis and modeling, company and industry research, preparing client presentations and interacting with senior bankers and clients.

Lazard offers an unparalleled opportunity to work as part of small client teams on major strategic assignments. We consider providing meaningful exposure to senior bankers and client representatives an important part of the analyst experience. Candidates should be top academic performers who are willing to work hard in an unstructured environment that values initiative, creativity, maturity and enthusiasm for learning. Academic backgrounds may vary so long as candidates are comfortable with financial concepts and enjoy quantitative work.

Summer Analysts

Summer Analysts typically join Lazard after completing their junior year of college. Our program provides those students considering a career in investment banking with an opportunity to explore the industry while making a real contribution to the Firm's success.

Summer analysts participate in an ongoing training program which includes classes taught by Lazard bankers. These sessions teach the fundamentals of investment banking with a particular emphasis on modeling and relevant analytical techniques. This training supplements the experience gained by working as part of active transaction teams.

How to Apply

For schools included in our Campus Events calendars, please check with your Careers Services office for specific application guidelines.

Interested investment banking candidates from all other schools should submit their cover letter and resume to:

Shannon Sullivan
Lazard Ltd.
30 Rockefeller Plaza
New York, NY 10020

Positions are available in New York, Atlanta, Chicago, Houston, Los Angeles, Montreal, San Francisco and Toronto.

No phone calls, e-mails or faxes please.

We strive to attract the best candidates based on ability, qualifications and business need.

This information is taken from publicly available sources.

Legg Mason Wood Walker, Inc.

100 Light Street
Baltimore, MD 21202
Phone: (877) 534-4627
Web site: www.leggmason.com

Locations

Baltimore, MD (HQ)
Chicago, IL
New York, NY
Philadelphia, PA
Washington, DC

In June 2005, Legg Mason Inc. agreed to swap its private client and capital markets units, including Legg Mason Wood Walker, for substantially all of Citigroup's asset management business; the deal is expected to close by the end of 2005.

The Stats*

Total Employees (2004): 5,250
Revenue (2004): $2.375 billion (gross revenues for calendar year 2004)

* These are stats for the parent company, Legg Mason, Inc., not Legg Mason Wood Walker

Employment Contact

www.leggmason.com/standout/working.htm

This information is taken from publicly available sources.

Legg Mason Wood Walker, Inc.

Employment Opportunities

For graduating seniors interested in the challenging world of investment banking, an analyst position at our firm is the ideal place to start. You'll begin your career in a two-year assignment handling the fundamental duties pivotal to the success of the investment banking deal-making process. Analyzing financial statements, creating financial models, updating market trends, developing forecasts and making presentations to clients. It's all a part of the high level of responsibility we expect from our analysts. And while it will demand your dedication and commitment, it will also push you to new levels of excellence.

College students looking to gain early experience with the demands and rewards intrinsic to investment banking need look no further than the Legg Mason Summer Internship Program. Here, you will be involved in all aspects of the business, encountering the challenges and contributing to the goals analysts and associates deal with on a daily basis.

Our interns are afforded the benefit of mentors to oversee their performance as they are rotated through the different industry groups and exposed to the diverse world of high finance. Representatives from senior management, research, institutional sales and other corporate segments will appear at weekly meetings to offer their insights into the work process. And you'll visit trading floors and our Philadelphia, Pennsylvania office for a first-hand take on our operations. Not to mention attending lunches, breakfasts and a variety of social events that will allow you to get to know your peers and learn from upper-level staff.

Excellent experience. An awesome working environment. And a staff of knowledgeable professionals that will support your endeavors at our firm. If the perfect indoctrination into investment banking is what you are searching for, then the Legg Mason Summer Internship Program will really stand out. Visit our college recruiting calendar on our web site to find out when we'll be conducting interviews on your campus.

Diversity Information

At Legg Mason, we maximize the strengths of multiple investment vehicles to help facilitate financial growth. We also seek to diversify our workforce to achieve the best results for our employees and our organization.

Legg Mason provides an environment that promotes respect, integrity, teamwork, achievement and acceptance regardless of race, gender, age, national origin, sexual orientation, religion, socio-economic status, education, job level, parental status, disability or marital status. We share a common value: responsiveness to our clients and to each other.

Diversity is the cornerstone of Legg Mason's future and we continue our initiatives to expand efforts to understand and promote diversity in our workplace, in our client relationships, in our industry, and in our communities. Web site address for diversity: www.leggmason.com/about/diversity.asp

This information is taken from publicly available sources.

Morgan Keegan & Co.

Morgan Keegan Tower
50 Front Street
17th Floor
Memphis, TN 38103
www.morgankeegan.com

Locations

145 offices in 15 states

The Stats

Total Employees (2004): 3,000
Revenue (2004): $ 727.2 million

Employment Contact

E-mail:
recruiting@morgankeegan.com

This information is taken from publicly available sources.

Employment Opportunities

Morgan Keegan offers many career opportunities in the fields of sales, trading, investment banking, technology, marketing and operations.

Many positions are offered through operations headquarters located in Memphis, Tennessee. Throughout our more than 240 locations, Morgan Keegan employs Financial Advisors who focus on the individual investor sector, or who serve institutional clients in either the equity or fixed income markets.

Throughout the Morgan Keegan system, paid internships are awarded to college students interested in gaining experience in the financial and investment industry

If you are interested in pursuing an internship opportunity with the Morgan Keegan headquarters in Memphis, TN, complete an online application and it will be submitted directly to the Human Resources department. Please indicate any specific areas of interest on your application. Web site address for employment: www.morgankeegan.com/html/blue/career_ops/default.asp

This information is taken from publicly available sources.

National City

1900 East Ninth Street
City: Cleveland, OH 44144
Phone: (216) 222-2000
www.nationalcity.com

Locations

1,100+ offices in the U.S.

The Stats

Total Employees (2004): 33,331
Revenue (2004): $10,559.9

Employment Contact

www.nationalcity.com/about/careers/default.asp

This information is taken from publicly available sources.

Employment Opportunities

National City offers exceptional career opportunities in a variety of fields. Backed by our Customer Champion promise – at National City, we care about doing what's right for our customers – we also extend that commitment to doing what's right for our employees.

Diversity Information

Diversity at National City is about inclusion.

Inclusion is embracing differences and similarities to fully utilize the talents of all for organizational success. Diversity supports our business agenda and promotes market growth by building inclusive relationships. Our business strategy of providing service excellence and strong returns through sustained market growth is integrally

linked to the effective delivery of our Customer Champion Brand promise, "at National City we care about doing what's right for our customers." Inclusive practices enhance our perspectives, our products, our team spirit and, ultimately, our ability to deliver superb performance. By applying a multi-cultural lens to the execution of our business practices, we live our brand. Our diversity strategy leverages the company as an economic resource to the employees, businesses and residents in the communities where we do business. By providing jobs, products and services, community investments and civic leadership, National City builds pathways to inclusion … one person, one relationship at a time. Web site address for diversity: www.nationalcity.com/about/Diversity/About/default.asp

This information is taken from publicly available sources.

Nomura Holdings

1-9-1 Nihonbashi, Chuo-ku
Tokyo 103-8011 JAPAN
Phone: +81-3-5255-1000

2 World Financial Center
Building B
New York, NY 10281
Phone:(212) 667-2310
www.nomura.com/Americas
E-mail: nomurajobs@us.nomura.com

Locations

Offices in the Americas, Asia and Europe

The Stats

Total Employees (2004) (U.S.): 979
Revenue (2004): $409.8 million

Employment Contact

www.nomura.com/Americas/
careers/index.shtml

This information is taken from publicly available sources.

Piper Jaffray

U.S. Bancorp Center
800 Nicollet Mall
Suite 800
Minneapolis, MN 55402
Phone: 612 303-6000
(800) 333-6000
www.piperjaffray.com

Locations

Minneapolis, MN (HQ)
Chicago, IL
Menlo Park, CA
New York, NY
San Francisco, CA
London

The Stats

Total Employees (2004):
Approximately 3,000
Revenue (2004): $797.5 million

Employment Contact

www.piperjaffray.com/info3.
  aspx?id=251

This information is taken from publicly available sources.

Employment Opportunities

We are committed to offering a stimulating environment and providing new and exciting opportunities and ongoing challenges to each individual at our firm. We are looking for individuals who pursue excellence and are highly motivated to succeed. The ability to critically analyze and problem-solve is an important characteristic, but we also value integrity, entrepreneurial spirit, energy, effective communication and client relationship skills.

The success of our business relies heavily on individuals and their ability to work closely in a team-driven environment. At the same time, the distinctive and unique strengths of each of our investment bankers and analysts are critical because these strengths continue to reshape our business and make Piper Jaffray the dynamic, exciting place it is.

Piper Jaffray is an Equal Opportunity Employer.

Contact Information

Please forward your resume and cover letter to:

Employment Services Representative
800 Nicollet Mall
Minneapolis, MN 55402-7020
800 333-6000
piperjaffray.recruitmax.com/ENG/candidates

This information is taken from publicly available sources.

Putnam Lovell NBF Securities Inc.

The Park Avenue Tower
65 East 55th Street
New York, NY 10022
Phone: (212) 546-7500
Fax: (212) 644-2271

Locations

New York, NY (HQ)
Boston, MA
San Francisco, CA
London

This information is taken from publicly available sources.

Employment Opportunities

Putnam Lovell NBF seeks exceptional candidates for all business areas, whether they are entry-level recruits or experienced professionals. If you wish to be considered for a position, please e-mail us your resume and cover letter indicating your area of interest and professional experience.

Internships

Putnam Lovell NBF has a limited number of summer internships available in our San Francisco, New York, and London Investment Banking practices. Responsibilities typically include:

- Financial analysis of mergers and acquisitions
- Preparation of offering memoranda
- Discounted cash flow and comparable company analysis supporting valuation opinions
- Preparation of business marketing presentations
- Research on industry transactions

If you are interested in being considered for an internship, please send your résumé and a cover letter indicating your interest in an internship as well as your office of preference. Web site address for employment: www.putnamlovell.com/index.asp

This information is taken from publicly available sources.

Raymond James Financial

880 Carillon Parkway
St. Petersburg, FL 33716
Phone: (727) 567-1000
www.rjf.com

Locations

More than 2,100 locations in:
North America
Asia
Europe
South America

The Stats

Total Employees (2004): 5,000
Revenue (2004): $ 1,829.8 million

Employment Contact

www.rjf.com/careers
E-mail:
employment@raymondjames.com

This information is taken from publicly available sources.

Employment Opportunities

The OPTIONS program provides recent college graduates with a number of unique opportunities that will help them understand how a successful firm operates in the financial services industry. Participants receive direction from the office of the chairman and benefit from direct contact with senior management.

Raymond James offers students a variety of summer internship opportunities. Each summer we place approximately 50 students in various positions throughout the company at our international headquarters in St. Petersburg, Florida. Many of our branch offices also offer internship positions.

Diversity Information

Raymond James is dedicated to an inclusive and diverse environment where differences are understood, respected and valued. Our commitment will enable us to successfully embrace the diverse markets we serve and capitalize on the talents of all our associates. This culture is the driving force behind our continued ability to put each client's financial well being first.

Diversity is our pledge to the clients and associates of Raymond James Financial.

This information is taken from publicly available sources.

RBC Capital Markets

Royal Bank Plaza
200 Bay Street
Toronto, Ontario M5J2W7
Phone: (416) 842-2000
Fax: (416) 842-8033
www.rbccm.com

Locations

60 offices in North America, Europe, Asia and Australasia

The Stats

Total Employees: approximately 59,549 (2005)

Employment Contact

www.rbc.com/uniquecareers
www.rbc.com/uniquecareers/
  diversity/index.html

This information is taken from publicly available sources.

Diversity Information

When we say diversity is one of our core values, it is not just rhetoric. We mean it. Our organizational history demonstrates support for our diversity strategies over a span of two decades. Early work with equal employment measures continues today and will do so until RBC workforce representation reflects the communities in which we work and live.

Over twenty years of diversity work have helped us understand how diversity enables us to meet our strategic priorities. By creating a workplace that is open and flexible, we want you to feel your ideas are seriously considered within your work environment. After all, encouraging innovative ideas is how organizations and its employees grow and achieve their goals.

As our workplace and markets change, we continue to build on our strong foundation of leveraging diversity. It's important because diversity provides the basis for behaviors we look for at RBC in serving our clients and in working with each other.

This information is taken from publicly available sources.

Robert W. Baird & Co. (Baird)

777 East Wisconsin Avenue
Milwaukee, WI 53202
Phone: (414) 765-3500
www.rwbaird.com

Locations

69 offices in the U.S. and Europe

Employment Contact

www.bairdcareers.com

This information is taken from publicly available sources.

Employment Opportunities

We are committed to making Baird a place where associates can thrive, both professionally and personally. Our tradition and culture – referred to as The Baird Way – define and differentiate us. It's the reason people come here. It's the reason people stay here.

With offices in the U.S. and four European countries, we provide individuals, corporations, institutional investors and municipalities a wealth of advice.

At Baird, we recognize that all our associates play an integral part in our growth and success.

This information is taken from publicly available sources.

Rothschild North America

1251 Avenue of the Americas, 51st Floor
New York, NY 10020
Phone: (212) 403-3500
Fax: (212) 403-3501
www.us.rothschild.com

Locations

40 offices in over 30 international cities including:

New York, NY (HQ)
London
Paris
Toronto
Tokyo
Singapore
Sydney

Employment Contact

www2.rothschild.com/graduates/us/article.asp?doc=articles/College University

E-mail: recruiting@us.rothschild.com

This information is taken from publicly available sources.

Employment Opportunities

Analysts

Analysts begin our program by participating in an intensive six-week training program covering topics from basic accounting to capital structures, credit, valuation and M & A modelling. Training also includes case study projects and presentations with senior bankers and training in London with the international class of analysts. During the two-year program, Analysts will focus on a broad range of corporate advisory and project financing assignments. Day-to-day responsibilities will include: financial analysis and modeling, company and industry research, preparing client presentations and contributing to team discussions and client meetings.

Qualifications

Due to the nature of our business being an independent platform, analysts are expected to assume high levels of responsibility at an early stage. Rothschild will consider candidates from all disciplines who have demonstrated both academic and professional achievement. The candidate should possess a high degree of maturity and self-confidence. Candidates should be highly motivated individuals with strong analytical, quantitative, writing and communication skills and computer literacy. Previous experience with basic accounting, finance and economic concepts is also helpful.

How to apply:
Campus Recruiter
Rothschild Inc.
1251 Avenue of the Americas
44th Floor
New York, NY 10020
recruiting@us.rothschild.com

This information is taken from publicly available sources.

Ryan Beck & Company

18 Columbia Turnpike
Florham Park, NJ 07932
Phone: (973) 549-4000
Fax: (973) 597-6414
www.ryanbeck.com

Locations

36 offices in 13 states

The Stats

Total Employees (2004): 1,255

Employment Contact

E-mail: jobs@ryanbeck.com

This information is taken from publicly available sources.

Employment Opportunities

Ryan Beck & Co., Inc. was founded in 1946 on the principles of offering high quality investments to meet client needs. Over 50 years of providing innovative financial solutions have followed, and the firm continues to focus its efforts on meeting its clients' long-term goals while meeting their short-term objectives.

The firm provides services to individuals, institutions and corporate clients through 36 offices in 13 states. For individual investors, the firm's Private Client Group (financial consulting) provides a full range of financial services, including investment consulting, retirement plans, insurance and investment advisory services. Institutional clients benefit from the market making, underwriting and distribution activities of the firm's experienced Capital Markets Group, which encompasses equity and fixed income trading, fixed income products, institutional sales and research. Through its Investment Banking Groups (financial institutions, middle market and public finance), Ryan Beck provides consulting and financial advisory services to corporate clients, primarily financial institutions and middle market companies. Ryan Beck's experience in this area is acknowledged industry-wide. Each of these areas complements the other, allowing the firm to provide superior service to its retail, institutional and corporate clients.

At Ryan Beck, we believe in teamwork, respect for others, in making the most of our time at work and in ensuring that our clients are well cared for. And we like to have fun while doing it!

Web site address for employment:
rbcoweb.ryanbeck.com/rbeck/careers/careers.asp

This information is taken from publicly available sources.

Sandler O'Neill

919 Third Avenue
6th Floor
New York, NY 10022
Phone: (212) 466-7800
Fax: (212) 466-7888
www.sandleroneill.com

Locations

New York, NY (HQ)
Atlanta, CA
Boston, MA
Chicago, IL
Memphis, TN
San Francisco, CA

This information is taken from publicly available sources.

Business Information

Sandler O'Neill was founded in 1988 with a single mission – to help financial institutions increase their franchise values through the execution of sound financial strategies. Today, Sandler O'Neill is one of the largest investment banking firms exclusively serving banks, thrifts, insurance companies and REITs.

We raise capital, provide research coverage, act as a market maker, advise on mergers and acquisitions, and trade securities for hundreds of clients nationwide. Our services extend to mutual-to-stock conversions, loan portfolio restructurings, strategic planning, and investment portfolio and overall balance sheet interest rate risk management.

From the beginning, we've based our success upon that of our clients. We firmly believe that our recommendations should be driven by an in-depth understanding of what is best for a client's business, and that our entire firm must work together to help clients achieve their goals.

Often, clients come to us with a specific need, but remain with us because we help them address many challenges. We, our partners and our dedicated colleagues, invite you to develop such a relationship with Sandler O'Neill.

This information is taken from publicly available sources.

SG Cowen & Co., LLC

1221 Avenue of the Americas
New York, NY 10020
Phone: (646) 562-1818

Locations

New York, NY (HQ)
Boston, MA
Cleveland, OH
Chicago, IL
Denver, CO
San Francisco, CA

Geneva
London

The Stats

Total Employees: 550

Employment Contact

www.sgcowen.com/
  CareerOpportunities.asp
E-mail: chip.rae@sgcowen.com

This information is taken from publicly available sources.

Employment Opportunities

Nearly 90 years of success on Wall Street, through every conceivable market environment, is a testament to SG Cowen's tradition of attracting and retaining highly talented people. The best people in any industry want to work for a firm that is committed to quality, engenders trust with its clients, encourages risk taking and rewards its people for creating and delivering successful ideas to its clients. SG Cowen continues to benefit from professionals being some of the most highly regarded individuals in their disciplines. Importantly, SG Cowen is large enough to provide every essential support to create success in one's chosen pursuit but is still of a size that an individual can make an impact on the firm's success.

SG Cowen actively recruits individuals from both the undergraduate ranks as well as the graduate ranks across the U.S, in the following areas:

Investment Banking
Be at the forefront of key growth industries, working to help you meet the financing and capital-raising needs of corporate clients.

Research
Join us for the rare opportunity to work alongside leading analysts in a number of today's fastest growing industries.

Institutional Sales & Trading
Join our team of sales and trading professionals and share their success based on depth of experience, strong client relationships and dedication to the business.

SG Cowen is an equal opportunity employer.

This information is taken from publicly available sources.

Stephens Inc.

111 Center Street
Little Rock, AR 72201
Phone: (501) 377-2000

Locations

18 in the U.S. and in London

Employment Contact

www.stephens.com/stephens/careers/
E-mail: HR@stephens.com

This information is taken from publicly available sources.

Employment Opportunities

The mission of Stephens Inc. is to become a trusted advisor to our clients in all aspects of their business and personal investments. We assist our clients as they interact with the financial markets, consider capital formation and preservation, and analyze strategic alternatives.

If you're interested in information about a career with Stephens Inc., contact us directly at:

PO Box 3507
Little Rock, AR 72203-3507
Fax: 501-377-2111
No telephone inquiries please

This information is taken from publicly available sources.

Susquehanna International Group

401 City Avenue
Suite 220
Bala Cynwyd, PA 19004
Phone: (610) 617-2600
Fax: (610).617-2689
www.susq.com

Locations

Bala Cynwyd, PA (HQ)
Boston, MA
Chicago, IL
New York, NY
Philadelphia, PA
San Francisco, CA

Dublin
Sydney

The Stats

Total Employees: 1,300

Employment Contact

www.susq.com/careers/

This information is taken from publicly available sources.

Employment Opportunities

Our employees are our most prized assets. Without them our success would not be possible. To ensure that we remain one of the leading participants in world markets, SIG actively fills its ranks with competitive, team-oriented candidates from diverse backgrounds.

Traits of the ideal candidate include the ability to work well under pressure, to use critical and non-linear reasoning and to communicate effectively with other team members. Relevant experience can include everything ranging from the football team to the debate team, from applied math to philosophy. Applicants undergo a unique interview process that focuses on skills that range from the quantitative to informed decision making.

SIG's culture and working environment challenge the individual and encourage teamwork. Our flat organizational structure rewards personal achievement, though even greater recognition is awarded to those who share their strengths with others.

At SIG, we recognize that as the markets evolve, so must the skills of our employees. We have therefore developed a formal educational curriculum that is widely recognized as one of the finest in the industry. SIG's comprehensive approach to training keeps us on the cutting edge of industry knowledge.

The growth of SIG's talent pool is critical to maintaining our leadership position. If you are a self-motivated person seeking a challenging work environment, we invite you to explore opportunities at SIG.

Susquehanna International Group, LLP is an Equal Opportunity Employer M/F/D/V.

Our on-campus presence at domestic and international universities has contributed greatly to our growth. While we obtain candidates for the Assistant Trader Program from a variety of different sources, career fairs and on-campus interviews have allowed us to cultivate relationships with organizations and students and receive a steady of flow of resumes and candidates.

If we do not actively recruit at the college you attend, use our online application system, or send a cover letter and resume to:

Susquehanna International Group, LLP
Recruiting Department
401 City Avenue
Suite 220
Bala Cynwyd, PA 19004

Thomas Weisel Partners

1 Montgomery Street
San Francisco, CA 94104
Phone: (415) 364-2500
Fax: (415) 364-2695
www.tweisel.com

Locations

San Francisco, CA (HQ)
Boston, MA
New York, NY
Palo Alto, CA

Employment Contact

www.tweisel.com/twpds?fwdtourl=/
 global/careers.jsp
E-mail: jobs@tweisel.com

This information is taken from publicly available sources.

Employment Opportunities

Thomas Weisel Partners is committed to a constant goal: industry leadership in financial services for the growth economy. Whether in a bear market or a bull market, we partner with our clients to provide insightful research and leading ideas specific to our growth focus.

At Thomas Weisel Partners, the culture is exciting, entrepreneurial and intense. Work is done in a team atmosphere, where creative thinking and individual initiatives are encouraged. Employees have direct interface with senior members of the Firm – a mentoring opportunity that is rare in larger firms.

We recruit self-motivators who are distinguished by their work experience, academic achievements and leadership accomplishments. We are looking for energetic individuals who possess self-confidence, strong written and verbal communication skills, and a winning attitude. You should be willing to work hard and contribute to the growth of our business.

If you are interested in a career at Thomas Weisel Partners, e-mail your cover letter and resume to jobs@tweisel.com. In the subject line of your e-mail, please specify to what department you are applying. If you prefer to send your information by mail, please use the following address:

Thomas Weisel Partners
Human Resources – Recruiting
One Montgomery Street, Suite 3700
San Francisco, CA 94104

This information is taken from publicly available sources.

Veronis Suhler Stevenson

350 Park Avenue,
New York, NY 10022
Phone: (212) 435-4990
Fax: (212) 381-8168
www.vss.com

Locations

New York, NY (HQ)
London

The Stats

Total Employees: 80

Employment Contact

www.vss.com/careers/carees home.html
E-mail: recruiting@vss.com

This information is taken from publicly available sources.

Employment Opportunities

Veronis Suhler Stevenson is a leading independent merchant bank solely dedicated to the media, communications and information industries. VSS offers its clients a unique skill set combining the knowledge and experience of media and communications industry executives and financial transaction professionals drawn from the ranks of such distinguished companies as: Time Warner, Merrill Lynch, Times Mirror, J.P. Morgan, CBS Publishing, First Boston, Westinghouse, Paine Webber, Credit Lyonnais, NBC, Hambrecht & Quist, Emmis Broadcasting, State Street Bank, IBM, BT Alex Brown, MCI, Chase Manhattan, Hachette Filipacchi, and Prudential Securities.

For questions regarding employment, please email us at recruiting@vss.com.

In addition, if you would like to be considered for an open position, please include your resume and salary history.

Director of Human Resources
Veronis Suhler Stevenson
350 Park Avenue
New York, New York 10022

This information is taken from publicly available sources.

WR Hambrecht + Co.

539 Bryant Street
San Francisco, CA 94107
Phone: (415) 551-8600

Locations

San Francisco, CA (HQ)
Boston, MA
Philadelphia, PA
New York, NY

Employment Contact

www.wrhambrecht.com/ind/about/employ/
E-mail: info@wrhambrecht.com

This information is taken from publicly available sources.

Employment Opportunities

WR Hambrecht + Co is an entrepreneurial full-service investment bank serving the financial services, software, Internet, healthcare, technology, real estate and branded consumer industries. The company was founded by Silicon Valley pioneer, William Hambrecht, and is active in investment banking, online brokerage services, private equity, mergers and acquisition advisory services, research, trading and underwriting. The firm has developed a number of innovative auction products, including OpenIPO, OpenFollowOn, and OpenBook to bring transparency, efficiency, and fairness to the capital formation process.

Please check our web site for current job openings.

This information is taken from publicly available sources.

GO FOR THE GOLD!

GET VAULT GOLD MEMBERSHIP AND GET ACCESS TO ALL OF VAULT'S AWARD-WINNING FINANCE CAREER INFORMATION

- **Employee surveys** on 100s of top finance employers with insider info on:
  - Firm culture
  - Salaries and compensation
  - Hiring process and interviews
  - Business outlook

- **Access to 100+ extended** insider finance employer profiles

- Complete access to **Vault's exclusive finance firm rankings**, including quality of life rankings

- Insider salary info with **Vault's Finance Salary Central**

- **Student and alumni surveys** for 100s of top MBA programs and law schools

- Receive Vault's **Finance Job Alerts** of top jobs posted on the Vault Finance Job Board

- Access to complete **Vault message board archives**

- **15% off** all Vault purchases, including Vault Guide and Finance Employer Profiles, Vault's Finance Interview Prep and Vault Resume Reviews (the WSJ's "top choice")

For more information go to
www.vault.com/finance

VAULT
> the most trusted name in career information™

About the Authors

About Vault

Vault is the leading media company for career information. The Vault Career Library includes 100+ titles for job seekers, professionals and researchers. Our team of industry-focused editors takes a journalistic approach in covering news, employment trends and specific employers in their industries. We annually survey 10,000s of employees to bring readers the inside scoop on industries and specific employers.

Popular Vault finance career titles include

- *Vault Guide to Finance Interviews*
- *Vault Guide to the Top 50 Banking Employers*
- *Vault Career Guide to Investment Banking*
- *Vault Career Guide to Investment Management*
- *Vault Career Guide to Hedge Funds*
- *Vault Career Guide to Sales & Trading*
- *Vault Career Guide to Venture Capital*

For a full list of titles, go to www.vault/com/finance

About SEO

SPONSORS FOR EDUCATIONAL OPPORTUNITY (SEO) is the nation's premier summer internship program for talented students of color. The SEO Career Program has expanded from 11 interns placed at four investment banks in 1980 to serving hundreds of exceptional students of color annually. SEO interns are placed in eight of the nation's most competitive industries, including investment banking, corporate law, asset management, global corporate finance, management consulting, information technology, accounting and philanthropy. Since its inception, the SEO Career Program has placed nearly 4,000 Black, Hispanic/Latino, Asian and Native American students in rigorous internships leading to full full-time job offers. In recent years, more than 80% of SEO Career Program interns have received job offers from SEO partner firms after their internships.

VAULT'S
DIVERSITY CENTRAL

The hub for workplace diversity information on Vault

Vault Corporate Diversity Profiles
Read about diversity initiatives at 100s of top employers

Vault Guides

- *Vault/INROADS Guide to Diversity Entry-Level, Internship and Co-Op Programs*
- *Vault/SEO Guide to Investment Bank Diversity Programs*
- *Vault/MCCA Guide to Law Firm Diversity Programs*
- *Vault Guide Conquering Corporate America for Women and Minorities*

Vault Employee Surveys
See what employees say about diversity at their employers

Expert career advice articles about corporate diversity issues

Go to www.vault.com/diversity

VAULT
> the most trusted name in career information™